"Ah done been tuh de horizon and back"

DEBRECENER STUDIEN ZUR LITERATUR

Herausgegeben von Tamás Lichtmann

Band 16

Herausgeberbeirat:

Kurt Bartsch, Graz
Árpád Bernáth, Szeged
Hans-Georg Kemper, Tübingen
Karl Müller, Salzburg
Thomas Schestag, Frankfurt/M.

Adresse des Herausgebers:

Universität Debrecen
Lehrstuhl für deutschsprachige Literatur
H-4010 Debrecen, Pf. 47
Ungarn

PETER LANG

Frankfurt am Main · Berlin · Bern · Bruxelles · New York · Oxford · Wien

Péter Gaál-Szabó

"Ah done been tuh de horizon and back"

Zora Neale Hurston's Cultural Spaces
in *Their Eyes Were Watching God*
and *Jonah's Gourd Vine*

PETER LANG
Internationaler Verlag der Wissenschaften

Bibliographic Information published by the Deutsche Nationalbibliothek
The Deutsche Nationalbibliothek lists this publication in the Deutsche Nationalbibliografie; detailed bibliographic data is available in the internet at http://dnb.d-nb.de.

ISSN 0946-1930
ISBN 978-3-631-61649-9

© Peter Lang GmbH
Internationaler Verlag der Wissenschaften
Frankfurt am Main 2011
All rights reserved.

www.peterlang.de

In toto

Acknowledgement

I deeply thank my mentor and friend, Professor Zoltán Abádi-Nagy, whose invaluable advice, insightful comments, and steadfast guidance contributed immensely to the process of researching and writing throughout the entire project.
I am also greatly indebted to my family, especially to my wife, my mother, and my grandparents, whose patience, support, and faith did not cease to serve as a motivating and nurturing background for my work.

Table of Contents

1. Introduction

Zora Neale Hurston has gone through many interpretations in the critical literature. Praised as an outstanding artist of the Harlem Renaissance and then neglected in her later life, Hurston died forgotten and in poverty (Hemenway 348). It was only later that Alice Walker, in her "In Search of Zora Neale Hurston," rediscovered and identified her as a significant literary forebear for contemporary African American woman writers. The reason for the renewed interest in Hurston on the side of the African American literary community can be found in a quest among African Americans for an African American literary tradition and for a distinct African American cultural identity.

The need for authentication detectable in the African American community voiced by Walker, but markedly manifested in the Harlem Renaissance renders Hurston's literary output relevant. Herself a writer and an anthropologist (a student of Franz Boas's), Hurston was as much a creative writer as a constant, participant observer of her own culture. This duality leads to a characteristic ambivalence in her fiction. As Barbara Johnson puts it, "she constantly tried to explain the difference between a reified 'art' and a living culture in which the distinction between spectator and spectacle, rehearsal and performance, experience and representation, are not fixed" (161). The blending of these seemingly distinct paradigms, the cultural and the literary, is in fact a means of subjectivation of the African American subject through African American culture, whereby Hurston manages to establish a cultural self in/through fiction in a dynamic way. Her cultural space contains and builds upon African American cultural artifacts in a playful, unfixed manner, and this technique pertains to including African American methodology of cultural inclusion. In this way, Hurston consciously employs a technique to revitalize her fictional subjects by recontextualizing and embedding them in an authentic cultural space rooted in African American cosmology and folk culture.

What justify the chosen theoretical foci of the present study are, on the one hand, the anthropological turn and a consequent emphasis on spatial thinking, signifying a shift away from traditional literary analyses; on the other hand, regarding the concrete analyses of Hurston's novels, validation can be found in Johnson's conceptualization of African American female identity. In her evaluation the black female can be conceptualized in the function of a "tetrapolar structure" (169), that is, in the cross-section of the binary pairs of black/white and male/female. The horizontal scale of gender and the vertical scale of race in Johnson's diagram represent two major lines in the function of which the black female is positioned. It is clear on the basis of Johnson's analysis of *Their Eyes Were Watching God* alone how both sexism and racism play an important role in Hurston's life and fiction. However, as regards the omnipresence of a racialized consciousness, I propose that Hurston's approach is not constructed by race but, first and foremost, by African American culture (much as race and culture are interrelated terms). The influence of Boasian cultural relativism serves as an explanation for it, but also Hurston's selfperception as revealed, for example, in her "How It Feels to Be Colored Me"—her appraisal of African American self. So while it is generally accepted by now that culture is, in fact, cultures (see Geert Hofstede's layers of culture [10]), the relevant aspects in Hurston's case are African American culture (to replace "race") and gender.

In the present study I intend to examine the dynamics of Hurston's cultural space in two of her novels, *Their Eyes Were Watching God* and *Jonah's Gourd Vine* (the two major novels that are regarded as the peak of her achievement in fiction), so as to show her method of engaging the dynamic interplay of space and place. The resulting richness and vitality of her novels denote a particular view of culture and an African American way of authentication that enable her to construct a fulfilling cultural universe for the individual, with/despite inbuilt tensions. The cultural space Hurston establishes is embedded in an African American cultural context associated with the South; at the same time, however, her cultural space proves to be diverse, due to inward heterogeneity and external contexts (e.g., a white socio-cultural frame).

In the two novels Hurston's different spatial paradigms unfold. I have chosen paradigms that are, perhaps, the most relevant and characteristic ones and play a singular role in revealing Hurston's cultural space: I will therefore deal with her Modernist "nonplaces"[1] that signify her cultural space especially in relation to the Harlem Renaissance, her religio-cultural space, as well as her gendered space.

In the first chapter, "The Concepts of Space and Place," I first focus on the meaning of space and place from two apparently contradictory angles. Much as the terms "space" and "place" appear to be unambiguous in an everyday sense, they must be problematized when it comes to theory. Reductive as it may seem, I distill the ways in which they are theorized into two opposing schools. One of them embraces an understanding of space, place, and the human subject as reflected in phenomenology: the human subject is emphasized and proves to be the center of place-construction. This bears special importance in African American cosmological discourse as selfassertion in an oppressive environment. The other theoretical school reflects a mainly post-Marxist delineation of space and place, but from a reverse point of view. It formulates the question how the human subject is produced by space or indoctrinated in place within a superimposed power structure. The constructive force of space is thus emphasized, and the role of the human subject in its cultural construction is de-

---

[1] See the chapter, "Black Cultural Space as Modernist Nonplace" for an elaboration of Marc Augé's concept of nonplace.

focalized. My chapter is an attempt to bring the phenomenological and post-Marxist paradigms together. Not that it is my aim to synthesize them; however, it can indeed be shown that thinkers of respective schools accommodate propositions of one another. What it all boils down to is that human subjects are able to hybridize space; that is, to appropriate and enliven it, despite embeddedness in a social/political/cultural context—a realization that proves to be an extremely important tool for the study of Hurston's multiple positionality in diverse racial, gender, class, or geographical discourses.

The second chapter, "Zora Neale Hurston: Cultural Space, and African American Spatiality," grounds my subsequent analysis of her cultural space in her two novels in relation to the major trend of Hurston scholarship. The popular focus on her vernacular use, as exemplified by Henry Louis Gates, Jr., and Houston Baker, does not at all override a concept of culture that permeates Hurston's lifework: they also examine Hurston's language use in terms of African American cultural phenomena, "signifying" and "blues performance," both of which reveal an important underlying cultural framework in African American literature. However, cultural awareness becomes even more significant in Hurston's case as she is also an anthropologist with a substantial record of field research in the South and the Caribbean. A genuine approach to Hurston and her fictional works thus necessitates a consideration of her anthropological research, her philosophy of culture, and an approach to her novels which is mindful of both anthropology and fiction. I will show that Hurston consciously blends both a traditionally African American and the anthropologist's writing strategy, adding her knowledge of African American cultural performances and places as well. The resulting cultural space is not a chaotic juxtaposition of methods and elements. Much rather, it reflects Hurston's principle of culture and revitalizes the African American hybridizing strategy, *tricksterism*, thereby refusing rigid conceptualization.

"Black Cultural Space as Modernist Nonplace" deals with Hurston's position regarding Black Modernism and the way that position permeates the construction of the novels. I introduce the label "nonplace" to indicate Hurston's dual distanced and mainstream position in the Harlem Renaissance. Relying on conceptualizations of nonplaces, I claim that, from the point of view of the black mainstream, Hurston occupies a position of difference informed by unique cultural politics. This, however, far from excluding her from Modernism, suggests solid situatedness in it. The trickster energy of her works itself can be seen as a Modernist trait, but also as recuperation to a cultural whole. Thus her works do not undermine the efforts of Black Modernism. The works bear this out: nonplaces prove to be constructing blocks in these works, never to debunk or deconstruct a social setting, but to underline it. Hurston's approach delineates a certain doubleness that works toward cultural inclusion along with sustained heterogeneity.

A similar cultural investigation follows in "Black Sacred Cosmos: Liminal Places and Hurston's Religio-Cultural Framework." Sacred places fulfill a similar function to nonplaces, but from a different point of view. Hurston's treatment of liminal places reveals African American cosmological understanding, a "black sacred cosmos" (see Lincoln and Mamiya [2]), as well as a dynamic pattern of anchoring the individual in the African American community. Liminal places signify sites of initiation that initially distance the individual from the community only to allow him/her to reemerge as its member. Hurston reevokes the anthropological category of liminality to dynamize her cultural space by reactualizing it (see Eliade [3]); that is, to revitalize subjectivity with a view of a unique African American cultural self.

Following the conceptual dichotomy established in the first chapter, I will divide my investigation of Hurston's gendered space into two inquiries. In "Gendered Space: Transparent Space, Female Social Space, and the Production of the Female Body" I will identify the gendered social space into which Hurston's female characters are placed. Employing feminist criticism, I propose that Hurston's gendered space is transparent, in which the female subject is trapped in a concerted interaction with male oppression. Female places are thus also gendered concerning their nature, structure, as well as their geographical placement. Such places are produced and maintained by the power mechanism of masculine social space, and, similarly, the female body is produced in/by these places. This framework does not only influence individual female subjects, but also determines the female social networks, producing a female version of transparent space. Much in the way dispositifs function (see Gilles Deleuze), female transparent space mediates power to socialize the female subject into place.

In "Female Places in Masculine Spaces: Hurston's Feminine Spatiality" my ultimate question is how Hurston's female subject is able to establish her individual places and space and to contribute to forming a communal space of women. I argue that Hurston's female subjects do retain subjectivity also through place-construction in two ways: a) by reinscribing space, whereby they use places of masculine social space to invert them into their own meaningful places; b) by establishing, what Teresa De Lauretis calls, "space off" (26). In this fashion, Hurston's women hybridize space, creating also a framework, where a genuine female communal space can evolve.

2. The Concepts of Space and Place

Before addressing African American understanding of spatiality in general and a possible interpretation of Hurston's cultural spaces in particular, it is necessary to delineate the main trends of spatial theory in the critical literature. In considering the relevance of, and significant contributions to, the academic discourse of space and place, I will subsequently ground my analysis in three focal points that also comprise the three parts of the present chapter. The first two parts are opposite in approach and in the resulting concept of the human subject, space, and place inhabited by that subject. I will also show that thinkers representing one school do not at all exclude propositions of the other. In fact, in the third part I will offer a balanced approach to the three discourses.

Phenomenologists, centering the world around the subject, endow the latter with the freedom to construct his/her subjective world. More concretely, it is the active subject's engagement that determines the nature of his or her surrounding world. In the first part I will focus on leading thinkers who have dealt with space and place and are considered by the critical literature to be the founding fathers of thinking about space and place. Because of the specific focus, I will have to omit relevant phenomenologists such as Edmund Husserl, Paul Ricoeur, and others, while being aware of their seminal contribution to phenomenology.

Marxist thinkers seek to show how the subject is *produced* by space, claiming that the human subject has a limited scope of action in his/her social environment. They position him/her in the focal point of discourses, such as the capitalist state, race, gender, or class, that determine the *quality* of action for the subject.

For Hurston, theoretical investigation bears special relevance, and my analysis of her cultural space will be based on these three theoretical strands. Even though Hurston is not a phenomenologist, she conceptualizes her subjects much in the line of phenomenological propositions; that is, she grants her subjects the potential to create their own places. Yet she is also aware of the limiting powers of the socio-cultural space—represented by post-Marxist thinkers in theory—which proves inhibiting for Hurston's subjects also. The third part of this chapter delineates a theoretical vista that can be seen as the acknowledgment of both schools—the way Hurston ultimately also approaches space: the in-between takes into consideration the properties and mechanisms of the socio-cultural space as well as the empowering capacities of the human subject.

2.1. The Phenomenology of Subject, Space, and Place

The groundbreaking philosophy that firmly established spatial thinking in modern thought was Martin Heidegger's. Several thinkers contributed significantly to exploring the subject's relation to space such as Immanuel Kant or Edmund Husserl, but it was Heidegger with his *Being and Time* to revolutionize Cartesian thought by defocalizing "the priority of knowledge over practice" (Dreyfus 19) in that, instead of maintaining the intense differentiation between *res cogitans* and *res extensa* characteristic of Western thought after Descartes (Lefebvre 406), he laid emphasis on human embededness.

Gjermund Wollan argues that Heidegger's conception of *Dasein* describes the stance of "an interested human being, situated in a particular place and a particular time" (33). Heidegger thus contextualizes *Dasein* in the temporality of the past-present-future of experience, as well as in its situatedness regarding social space. In fact, Heidegger explicitly claims that *Dasein* is spatial (*Being* 111), "but Da-sein is 'in' the world in the sense of a familiar and heedful association with the beings encountered in the world. Thus when spatiality is attributed to it in some way, this is possible only on the basis of this being-in. But the spatiality of being-in shows the character of *de-distancing and directionality*" (105). *Dasein* experiences itself *thrown in the world*, which is an always already being-in-the-world, and the subject knows the world as the subject knows him/herself, so s/he encounters this known world as totality. The world of the subject, however, is not stable: the existentials, de-distancing and directionality, show exactly that *Dasein* is always in motion in that, on the one hand, it becomes conscious of itself in a reflective manner (as it interprets and reinterprets itself) and, on the other, it gets to know the surrounding world as it attaches the world to itself. For Heidegger the spatial metaphor of de-distancing denotes *Dasein*'s absorbing character via (self-)interpretation, while directionality presupposes for him *Dasein*'s "prereflective basis" (Wollan 33). As Heidegger explains,

> The handiness which belongs to each region beforehand has as the being of what is at hand the *character of inconspicuous familiarity* in a more primordial sense. The familiarity itself becomes visible in a conspicuous manner only when what is at hand is discovered circumspectly in the deficient mode of taking care of things. [. . .] Space, which is discovered in circumspect being-in-the-world as the spatiality of a totality of useful things, belongs to beings themselves as their place. (*Being* 104)

Prereflection orders things into their place. It, in fact, refers to *Dasein*'s reflective filter of the world that renders things as handy; it is its filter of perception that dynamically creates continuation for *Dasein* in space and time, ensuring *Dasein*'s dynamic temporality of past-present-future. Prereflective approach is responsible for the interpretation of the Heideggerian present-at-hand ("vorhandene") as ready-to-hand ("zuhandene"), which means, on the one hand, a horizon of interpretation induced by past experiences, and, on the other hand, practically a constant coming-to-know of things as well as their meaningful emplacement into *Dasein*'s world. The dynamic continuity resulting from this kind of dwelling is responsible for the subject's sense of place, which, then, does not only reflect a geographical constraint, but also a temporal one. In fact, time and place must be interwoven in this sense, as only in the function of past-present-future can the intentionality of different entities be understood.

For Heidegger the objective, geometrical world cannot be detected as "[objective] space is still veiled in the spatiality of what is at hand" (104). The ready-to-hand expresses exactly the domestication of objective space by *Dasein*; that is, entities can only exist for *Dasein* if contextualized in *Dasein*'s system. In an interconnected mode, *Dasein* is also embedded in this space, while it shapes space as space's centre. *Dasein* in Heidegger's interpretation is the point of departure for any exploration of the surrounding world. As he explains, "[t]his world is always already from the outset my own" (118), and "the world at hand [is] where *Dasein* dwells in *taking care*" (119); so the space disclosed around *Dasein* belongs to *Dasein*'s spatiality, and *Dasein* relates to this known world with active engagement and familiarity (see Critchley 160, Wollan 37). *Dasein*'s spatiality denotes two things: for one, *Dasein* is thrown into the world (objective space veiled over) in the manner of always already being-in-the-world along with other entities ("being-there-too with them" [*Being* 118], "Mitda-sein" [119]), establishing *Dasein* as a temporal-spatial entity, which has an objective quantifying character such as the body; and, secondly, it refers to the spatiality of the ready-to-hand evolving around *Dasein* including itself (118).

Heidegger breaks spatiality into smaller units. Place gains meaning not only as position of an object somewhere as a part of totality: "The actual place is defined as the place of this useful thing for [. . .] in terms of a totality of the interconnected places of the context of useful things at hand in the surrounding world" (103); but place has the essential character of belongingness. This suggests relatedness to other entities, as well as, in the function of de-distancing and directionality, place also expresses "whereto" (103)—a term denoting for Heidegger the contextualization of places in a broader spatiality, which is part of *Dasein*'s spatiality:

> We call this whereto of the possible belonging somewhere of useful things, circumspectly held in view in advance, and heedful association, the *region*. [. . .] The kind of place which is constituted by direction and remoteness—nearness is only a mode of the latter—is already oriented

toward a region and within that region. Something akin to a region must already be discovered if there is to be any possibility of referring and finding the places of a totality of useful things available to circumspection. This regional orientation of the multiplicity of places of what is at hand constitutes the aroundness, the being around us of beings encountered initially in the surrounding world. (103-4)

Region refers thus to the texture of places and, likewise, place reflects the directionality of *Dasein*'s spatiality that comes to expression in region. "Region is linked to our use associated with things, ready-to-hand. In this way, region forms a limited action and tools context" (Wollan 36); that is, region embraces the different functions and objects of the different places. Furthermore, region also denotes, besides, directionality, interrelation between places. As Eugene Francis Kaelin claims, "the tool's placement is fixed with respect to a definite direction: there, relative to a certain here *(dort und da)* established by a human being's involvement of itself in its environment. The hither point and the thither point of the relationship create a region, which is the actual 'whither' of the human involvement in its world" (82-83).

Heidegger's approach to being is a very practical one in fact. He represents *Dasein* as the node of being, and *Dasein*'s spatiality refers not only to its body as spatial form, but also as a prereflective scope of semantization of things; subjects thus dwell in the place-world with an inert understanding of the surrounding world. Familiarity with the world is the way the world comes into being for the subject, that is, the way the subject encounters and makes sense of the surrounding world through his/her place-world.

Heidegger's understanding is also touched upon and enlarged on by other thinkers. Jean-Paul Sartre emphasizes the embodied experience, for whom the subject cannot be severed from the body. He speaks of the body as both object as well as "contingent form" and "for-itself" *(Being and Nothingness* 408). Sartre understands the subject as embodied subject, which "must be wholly body and it must be wholly consciousness" (404). This is why it is through that body the subject maintains a relation with the world. The world, or space, for Sartre, as for Heidegger, is hidden as an "indefinite multiplicity of reciprocal relations [. . .] and can not even be represented" (405). It is Being-for-itself (Sartre's coinage of what Heidegger calls *Dasein*, and what is the embodied subject for Merleau-Ponty) that renders order in the world by being the point of reference in the world: "[the] world can not exist without a univocal relation to me" (406). The relation between the world and the subject is established through the subject's "engaged knowledge" (407), which is the "only engaged upsurge in a determined point of view which one *is*" (407).

The embodied subject and his/her lived experience gain also relevance in Merleau-Ponty's philosophy: for him "[t]he body itself is the perceiving subject:

the point of view of the world, the time-space structure of the perceiving experience" (Sadala 286). Materializing *Dasein* as phenomenal body (see Marcoulatos 2) in this way, he emplaces the body in the world similarly to the spatiality of Heidegger's *Dasein*. The embodied subject, through its "motor intentional activity" (Kelly 386)[2], explores the surrounding in a "spatiality of situation" (*Phenomenology* 100). Thereby understanding is not rendered a function of form (Aravot 209), but one of emplacement in time and place and of the body's intentionality. As Merleau-Ponty elaborates in *Phenomenology of Perception*:

> Now the body is essentially an expressive space. [. . .] The body is our general medium for having a world. Sometimes it is restricted to the actions necessary for the conservation of life, and accordingly it posits around us a biological world; at other times, elaborating upon these primary actions and moving from their literal to a figurative meaning, it manifests through them a core of new significance: this is true of motor habits such as dancing. Sometimes, finally, the meaning aimed at cannot be achieved by the body's natural means; it must then build itself an instrument, and it projects thereby around itself a cultural world. (146)

Spatializing the subject through embodiment, Merleau-Ponty imposes restrictions by the body on the subject, not only physically, but regarding the interpretation of the world. As Kelly points out, bodily activity seems some time independent of the subject's will (390), as if the subject acted unconsciously. However, Merleau-Ponty identifies the body as the mediator between self and the world, where the self gets the upper hand in giving meaning to its environment by using and transforming the surroundings.

In a similar manner, Gaston Bachelard conceives of place through the inhabiting practice of the subject. When considering the subject's creative imagination, he claims, "the soul comes and inaugurates the form, dwells in it, takes pleasure in it" (xviii), creating a "*felicitous space*" (xxxi). Imagination as conceptualized by Bachelard appears very similar to Heidegger's idea of *Dasein*'s spatiality. For Bachelard "the original and miraculous leap of the spirit" (Thiboutot par. 25) interprets any work of art, that is, any phenomena it encounters in the world. In this way, subjects establish an original space of dwelling: "Space that has been seized upon by imagination cannot remain indifferent space subject to the measures and estimates of the surveyor. It has been lived in, not in its positivity, but with all the partiality of the imagination" (Bachelard xxxii). Negating the integrity of objective space in the encounter

---

[2] Sean Dorrance Kelly explains that in the Merleau-Pontian understanding motor intentionality has motor and behavioral aspects and the way it relates to objects reflects the understanding of these aspects (386).

with the perceiving subject comes more to the foreground in his discussion of the house: "the house image would appear to have become the topography of our intimate being [. . .] [B]y remembering 'houses' and 'rooms,' we learn to abide within ourselves [. . .] [T]he house image moves in both directions: they are in us as much as we are in them" (xxxiii). Time and space in Bachelardian epistemology build an organic unity with the subject. As in Heidegger and Merleau-Ponty, this does not only mean that the subject determines the *genius loci*,[3] but also that the subject is emplaced in a particular temporal-spatial paradigm: the subject responds to the challenges of the surrounding world in the function of his/her own temporal-spatial history.

It is clear on the basis of these thinkers that the subject's temporal-spatial structuring of spatiality is inherently an active and practical one, not detached from the environment, but embedded in it. Edward Casey, among others, establishes the link between the subject and his/her environment by, what he calls, "habitus."[4] On the one hand, similarly to Merleau-Ponty, Casey identifies the body as the link between the self and "lived place" ("Geography" 683); on the other, he insists on a "core of habitudes" (686), something that connects place with the geographical self. Merleau-Ponty addresses this issue through the differentiation of the visibility of the body and the invisibility of what is beyond (before) the body, the "latent content of the past" and the "elsewhere" (*Visible* 114). In fact, he too suggests that there must be something beyond the limitation of the body in time and space that is responsible for the continuation of the embodied self in these two strata in the visible temporal-spatial structuring materialized in, around, and by the body. He expands his concept of the lived body to an idea of a "spatial and temporal pulp" that goes beyond a presentism and materiality of the body, to allow also an intentionality shaped by habitus.

Habitus is the practical understanding of Heidegger's prereflectivity of *Dasein* as it grants the scheme of understanding of any place as well as the continuity of the subject in other places: "A given habitus is always enacted in a particular place and incorporates the features inherent in previous such places, all of which are linked by a habitudinal bond" (Casey, "Geography" 686). Habitus provides the subject with a temporal-spatial reality; that is, past experiences, places, and habitus dynamically condition the subject's present habitus and action, while through the habitudinal bond the continuity of

---

[3] Christian Norberg-Schulz's *Genius Loci* describes the phenomenon by which the place is endowed with meaning, transcending geometrical form (see Thomson).

[4] Wollan reminds us that Heidegger uses this term he borrows from Thomas Aquinas to "describe[] people's association with everyday objects" (32). Pierre Bourdieu also has an important contribution to the concept of habitus. I will address his definition in the chapter "Hurston's Gendered Space."

historicity is ensured. Habitus is, thus, also directly connected to the subject's intentionality as it is the underlying motor of directionality as well as the realization of intentionality in a particular place.

Casey emphasizes the body's role in place-making. Reminiscent of Merleau-Ponty, Casey claims that "habitus is composed precisely of bodily schemata," thus emphasizing "bodily engagement" ("Habitus" 716) in place-creation: "Only the body holds together, in one coherent entity, the sense of place, the past pertinent to that place (that is, via body memories), and the orienting power which place requires" (718). Casey thus places the body in the centre of place as the entity that gives place temporal and spatial stability.

This becomes more explicit in his book *Remembering: A Phenomenological Study*, in which he distinguishes two concepts of the body: body as intra-place and body as inter-place. In fact, he identifies two—the vertical and horizontal—aspects of the lived body. Body as intra-place establishes that the body is the organizing force in a given place; every object gains its place through the ordering of the body: "the body as intra-place is thus a place *through* which whatever is occurring in a given setting can take place: it is a place of passage for such occurrences" (196). Placing does not only signify a mere selection here, but also meaningful placing in relation to the body as a "place of anchoring" (196). Body as inter-place, on the other hand, denotes for Casey the connective aspect of the body as "[t]he lived body creates the inter-place in which the two epicenters of the here and the there are brought into concrete connection" (196). Different places are brought together in the place-world by the subject's movement between and through them.

The subject absorbs place through habitus-directed bodily activity, in other words, by transforming place to the subject's own likeness. Places become dwelling-places, places of habitation. As shown before, Bachelard conceptualizes the home as the expression of the subject's being. In fact, studying the home can be seen as the mapping of the self of the subject. Similarly, Emmanuel Levinas sees habitation as "the outpouring of consciousness in things, which does not consist in a representation of things by consciousness, but in a specific intentionality of concretization" (153). Concretization corresponds to place-making in practice. However, habitation is not a detached or isolated process because subjects are always-already (fallen and thrown—to use Heidegger's coinage) in the world, which is why "the consciousness of a world is already consciousness *through* that world. [Thus] the subject contemplating the world presupposes the event of dwelling, the withdrawal from elements [. . .], recollection in the intimacy of the home" (153).

Heidegger maintains a resembling notion of habitation when he claims that "to build is in itself already to dwell" ("Building" 146). For him dwelling is also an active phenomenon, which he compares to cultivating (147). Indeed, this word expresses not only maintenance, but also active engagement and transformation, or, rather, realization. Or, as he points out through the metaphor of the bridge, dwelling is like gathering or assembling of things in a unique way (153). As being for Heidegger is always being-in-the-world, the act of gathering is always with relation to the centralizing *Dasein*—again as he claims about the bridge: "But only something *that is itself* a location can make space for a site" ("Building" 154).

The centralizing activity, which can be equated with habitation, draws things and relations around itself in an ordered way. This may be seen as the procreation of places, however, Casey insists that there is also an active interaction between self and place responsible for the maintenance of places, an interaction that belongs to the chemistry of places: "the self relates to the place of habitation by means of concerted bodily movements that are the activation of habitudinal schemes, their explication and exfoliation in the inhabited place-world" ("Geography" 687). The body as location and centralizing agent inhabits the place through bodily activity motivated by habitus. In this way, places become places of stability in as much the self can be seen as stable. As Casey claims elsewhere: "In the actions of the customary body, then, we observe the continuance of time in place–a continuance that connotes not merely maintenance but active incorporation" (*Remembering* 194). That is, habitation denotes that place is organically interdependent with the subject from a phenomenological point of view, and it directly follows the dynamic changes in the subject's habitus.

In phenomenological understanding the heart of the world is the self. It is, however, always placed somewhere; thus the self has not only a temporal, but also a spatial aspect. The self goes out and meets the world (even though always-already in the world), in a sense creates it by giving it meaning. The self appears as the active agent that grants the world as totality (the world encountered by the subject) and stability. Stability or continuance can only be conceptualized in the function of the self's matrix of spatiality and temporality. The concept of habitus conveys well the intentionality of the subject in practice. It suggests the structuring force of bodily activity based on the experiences of the past. Habitus corresponds, in fact, to the process of selection, simplification, and idealization of experiences, setting up a horizon of how to act in a given place. In the place/self interaction the active interface is the lived body that enforces habitus as well as responds to the place's challenges for the subject's habitudinal schemes by incorporating them by way of negation or adoption. In this way, the subject through his/her habitus-directed bodily activity inhabits the place.

2.2. Post-Marxist Geography: The Production of the Human Subject in Space and by Place

Despite the overwhelming focus on the subject's ability to be the agent of place-making in phenomenological thinking, the presence of some external or internal structuring force cannot be discounted. Even the thinkers discussed so far cannot exclude a force that prevents the subject's complete control over him/herself and the surrounding world. Just as Merleau-Ponty yields some control to the body over the subject through his concept of motor intentionality, Heidegger too problematizes *Dasein*'s conceptualization. The concept of "anxiety" in Heidegger's philosophy can be taken as a disturbance that allows for the possibility of the (spatial) production of the subject. Anxiety is a state in which *Dasein* realizes its fallenness in the world as a constant challenge to cope with. This means that "Anxiety [. . .] takes away from *Dasein* the possibility of understanding itself" (Wollan 34); as well as it enhances *Dasein*'s ability to overcome dynamically the gap between fallenness and authenticity. Steve Kirby reminds us: "The choice with which we are faced is stark; to embrace our freedom and potentiality for authentic existence through the overcoming of our anxiety. Or to refuse or ignore anxiety's challenge and succumb to the 'they-self'" (75).[5]

For Heidegger, authenticity lies in *Dasein*'s ability to establish *Dasein*'s spatiality, and that despite all temporal, socio-cultural or other conditions. However, as Critchley puts it, "I project or throw off a thrownness that catches me in its throw and inverts the movement of possibility" (168). Critchley highlights *Dasein*'s situatedness in time and space, more specifically, *Dasein* finds its place in their function.

The notion of binding situatedness appears also in Sartre's philosophy as "practico-inert ensemble" (*Critique* 313). In his *Critique of Dialectical Reason* he discusses at one point people queuing up at a bus stop creating a social product and thus "a movement towards the interchangeability of men and of the instrumental ensemble" (313). The metaphor of the bus stop serves him to show how totalization is achieved on both individual and group level. Through "serial behaviour, serial feelings and serial thoughts" (321) a certain praxis is called into being that is also serial. Such "a series is a mode of being for individuals both in relation to one another and in relation to their common being and this mode of being transforms all their structures" (321). Ultimately, not only the minds and behavior of people are affected, but their movement becomes structured in the function of "practico-inert ensembles," as well as their places

---

[5] Kirby seems to admit, however, an overdetermination toward the former possibility: "anxiety fulfils a positive function by summoning us to take up the challenge of authentic existence" (75).

become practico-inert space and abstract space (see Boyle). In this way, individuals, groups, and their places get integrated into an overarching context. As Sartre writes,

> Conversely, in every non-serial praxis, a serial praxis will be found, as the practico-inert structure of the praxis in so far as it is social. And, just as there is a logic of the practico-inert layer, there are also structures proper to the thought which is produced at this social level of activity; in other words, there is a rationality of the theoretical and practical behaviour of an agent as a member of a series. (*Critique* 321)

For Sartre any group becomes a practico-inert ensemble that eliminates opposition and effects homogeneity. This is also true for groups that initially aim at detotalisation of a particular practico-inert ensemble: "It must therefore be understood *at the outset* that the origin of any restructuration of a collective into a group is a complex event which takes place *simultaneously* at every level of materiality, but is transcended into organising *praxis* at the level of serial unity" (329). As also shown by Boyle, Sartre's circular dialectic is expressed exactly through this movement: a group that reasserts itself in opposition to an oppressive, practico-inert context is going to turn into one too, as it also works toward a practico-inert unity.

Neither does Bachelard's interpretation of the subject and space appear homogeneous. He admits that in all of us there exists an "oneiric house" (15): "the house we were born in has engraved within us the hierarchy of the various functions of inhabiting. We are the diagram of the functions of inhabiting that particular house, and all the other houses are but variations on a fundamental theme" (15). Following Bachelard's interpretation this can mean two things: either there is a house the subject is initially positioned in, which leaves lasting, unwanted imprints on the subject; or the inhabitation of the first house provides the subject with a directionality, which is responsible for the subject's intentionality, or as Casey calls it: habitus. Either way, the subject experiences a conditioning, external or internal, which must then entail a fundamental restriction on possibilities.

Casey's concept of space as "the encompassing volumetric void in which (including human beings) are positioned" ("Geography" 683) is also revealing. This can be taken as the general argument for space to be an overall container. However, the idea of positioning conveys yet the lack of at least some degree of agency. From another angle, such conceptualization of space can refer to the existential notion of being-in-the-world, in which case Casey's argument describes the subject's thrownness in the world. Nevertheless, he admits more concretely the subject's dependence on place elsewhere: "unless [the body] feels oriented in place, *we* as its bearers are not going to feel oriented there either

[and] certainly experience *Heimatlosigkeit*" (*Remembering* 195). Similarly to Heidegger and his idea of anxiety, Casey argues for the subject's dynamic habitation of place, yet he also anticipates the interdependence of subject and place.

Casey also emphasizes—besides the "outgoing" of the subject ("Geography" 688), that is, the way the subject actively confronts the surrounding—the process of "incoming" (688), which for Casey denotes the effect places have on the subject. This "somatography," or "inscription" of places in the body (688) is reminiscent of Bachelard's idea of the oneiric house, when Casey links it up with the tenacity of places. What is more in contrast with the aforesaid is his concept of subjection to place (688); as he claims: "we are not the masters of place but prey to it [. . .] to be (a) subject to/of place is to *be what we are as an expression of the way a place is*" (688).

In a more radically opposing way to phenomenologists, many thinkers emphasize the production of subjects in space. This term suggests that subjects cannot build, or construct their places apart from discursive powers, if construction, that is, a degree of individualism, can be assumed as a possibility at all. In contrast with the phenomenological understanding, post-Marxist thinkers lay emphasis on the determining (socio-political, etc.) environment, in which the embedded "subject" is intensely conditioned. As Michel Foucault stresses it, "The individual, with his identity and characteristics, is the product of a relation of power exercised over bodies, multiplicities, movements, desires, forces" ("Questions on Geography" 74). Similarly to subjects, spatiality appears also in the focal point of power relations. As Edward W. Soja reminds us, many of these thinkers maintain that "spatial fragmentation as well as the appearance of spatial coherence and homogeneity are social products and often an integral part of the instrumentality of political power" (*Postmodern Geographies* 126).

As in the case of the thinkers in the first part of this chapter, in addition to time, space becomes seminal here too. It must be mentioned that Mikhail Bakhtin addressed the relation between space and time even before, in the first place, Foucauldian thinkers to be discussed in this chapter. In *The Dialogic Imagination* he introduces the concept of the *chronotope* in the study of the novel: "a formally constitutive category of literature. . .[in which] spatial and temporal indicators are fused into one carefully thoughtout, concrete whole. Time, as it were, thickens, takes on flesh, becomes artistically visible; likewise, space becomes charged and responsive to the movements of time, plot and history" (84).[6] The chronotopic concurrence of space and time—the palpability of time in space and the amoebic character of space in time—stresses the relevance of spatial analysis.

---

[6] Bakhtin introduces other spatial terms such as the "zone of contact" (7) to describe, for example, the function of laughter in literature (23). Bakhtinian analysis has also been employed by anthropologists. Notably, Keith Basso studies Western Apache landscape,

Foucault also recognizes the importance of spatial analysis as it allows for "grasp[ing] precisely the points at which discourses are transformed in, through and on the basis of relations of power" ("Questions on Geography" 70). In Foucault's footstep, Soja adds:

> Just as space, time, and matter delineate and encompass the essential qualities of the physical world, spatiality, temporality, and social being can be seen as the abstract dimensions which together comprise all facets of human existence. [. . .] [t]he social order of being-in-the-world can be seen as revolving around the constitution of society, the production and reproduction of social relations, institutions, and practices. (*Postmodern Geographies* 25)

In such analyses the social being can be understood in specific circumstances in the intersection of time and matter, which involves abstract and direct spatiality—engendered by clandestine relations of power and immediate places in which bodies are positioned.

Despite the relatively meager quantity of spatial/geographical investigations Foucault makes in contrast to his other enterprise, he is straightforward about power relations in space:

> This form of power applies itself to immediate everyday life which categorizes the individual, marks him by his own individuality, attaches him to his own identity, imposes a law of truth on him which he must recognize and which others have to recognize in him. It is a form of power which makes individuals subjects. ("The Subject and Power" 212)

The immediacy Foucault talks about allows one to consider different places as "forms of domination" ("Questions on Geography" 69), and, as such, they become intersections of power relations and thus sites of exercising power. In this way, places for Foucault are sites of reproduction, where the "active subject" comes into being by way of approval or disapproval ("The Subject and Power" 220).

The term "production" often used in this academic realm enhances best the decentering of the subject and the approach to space. Certainly it is not by chance that Henri Lefebvre gave his intriguing work the title *The Production of Space*. He claims right at the beginning that "*(social) space is a (social) product*" (Lefebvre 26), whereby he claims—similarly to Heidegger—that space

---

especially place names, as "a repository of distilled wisdom (63) to show that as "inhabitants *of* their landscape, the Western Apache are. . .inhabited *by* it as well, and in the timeless depth of that abiding reciprocity, the people and their landscape are virtually as one" (102).

does not appear as an apriori entity[7]; rather, he speaks about "appropriated space" which is produced: "every society-and hence every mode of production with its subvariants [. . .] produces a space, its own space" (Lefebvre 31). Appropriated space, as if concealed, appears in Lefebvre's interpretation in the function of a twofold illusion of transparency and reality—homogeneity [as Lefebvre says, space seems "intelligible" (27)] and materiality for "its appeal to naturalness [and] substantiality" (29). Lefebvre thus connects space to both conception and perception.

In fact, what Lefebvre proposes is a conceptual triad in his analysis that directly connects to the conception and perception of space. *Spatial practice* does not only entail action to maintain production and reproduction, but also sites, thereby securing "continuity [and] cohesion" (33). *Representations of space* are connected to knowledge, whereas *representational spaces* embody "complex symbolisms" (33). Lefebvre's triad allows many interpretations, so, for example, Jay D.Gatrell and Jeff Worsham represent spatial practice as the glue between the two spaces, thus conceptualizing with this triad the easing of the tension of the traditional binary pair of place and space: "spatial practices transform imagined geographies defined as 'representations of space' (i.e. space) into the materiality of everyday life as constituted in 'representational spaces' (i.e. place)" (335). In his analysis of race and space Eugene J. McCann represents the "triad of conceived, perceived, and lived spaces" (167)[8] as "Lefebvre's three moments [to] capture bodily experiences toward space and therefore [to] suggest that the racially 'marked' bodies will have a particular relationship to, and constitutive role in, the production of abstract spaces which always attempt to elide difference" (179). David Harvey's conceptualization of Lefebvre's triad enlarges on this understanding more systematically. For him spaces of representation "imagine new meanings or possibilities for spatial practices" (219); thus Harvey understands these spaces as challenging, destabilizing—if not subverting—representations of space which he sees as organized space including architecture and (spatial) knowledge. Spatial practices are material and physical that "assure production and social reproduction" (218). In this way, spatial practices occur as supporting tools of representations of space in the first place. He identifies representations of space as a "material productive force with respect to spatial practices" (219).[9]

---

[7] In fact, if space *per excellence* can be equated with nature void of, e.g., enculturation, Lefebvre argues that natural space is disappearing and has become a mere background (30). In this sense, Lefebvre echoes Heidegger about the hiddenness of space.

[8] In *The Production of Space* this appears as "the perceived-conceived-lived triad (in spatial terms: spatial practice, representations of space, representational space)" (40).

[9] Derek Gregory underscores this understanding with an overtly Foucauldian tinge: spatial pracitce enhances for him "time-space routines and the spatial structures [. . .] through which social life is produced and reproduced"; he identifies representations of space as

Indeed, as Lefebvre explains, the three moments are interwoven, but representations of space as "conceptualized space" (38) are "dominant space" (39), to which subordination to a logic (41) is inherent. This notion of representations of space connects directly to Lefebvre's other concept of *abstract space*, which is "formal and quantitative, and [. . .] erases distinction" (49). Quite contrary to Gatrell and Worsham's proposition, unless interpreted in terms with abstract space, the (political) technology of abstract space influences the realizations of the two other moments of Lefebvre's triad. Lefebvre explicitly talks about the conditioning of the subject in space (57) and, as regarding space, he states that "abstract space generates illusions, and hence a tendency towards false consciousness, i.e., consciousness of a space at once imaginary and real" (411). Abstract space represents a political technology, both as its product and instrument, that creates a transparent, homogenous space. Uniformity of space is obtained through "consensuses" validated by a "political economy" (56) and, as McCann points out, by "render[ing] [it] ahistorical, devoid of any indications of the social struggles around its production, or traces of the concrete space it replaces" (169). Ahistoricity of abstract space and the lack of social struggle must mean, however, the denial of alternative and challenging histories from the point of view of the dominant discourse—the handling of space by, first and foremost, engendering false consciousness. As Lefebvre states:

> In *spatial practice*, the reproduction of social relations is predominant. The *representation of space*, in thrall to both knowledge and power, leaves only the narrowest leeway to *representational spaces*, which are limited to works images and memories, whether sensory, sensual or sexual, is so far displayed that it barely achieves symbolic form. (50)

(Social) action and any individual construction are conditioned by social space; they can be seen as products, just as social space is a product of power relations. This connects Lefebvre's theory directly to Foucault's theory of space. Production and reproduction—management and maintenance of space—appears to be a part of a power mechanism.

These power frameworks appear in Harvey's theory as "time-space compressions"—"processes that so revolutionize the objective qualities of space and time that we are forced to alter, sometimes in quite radical ways, how we represent the world to ourselves" (240). Harvey's definition has two implications. First, space is not stable but subject to change enforced by socio-political-economic power mechanisms. (In fact, Harvey discusses periods of

---

"constellation of power, knowledge, and spatiality—in which the dominant social order is materially inscribed"; in contrast, spaces of representation is regarded by him as "counterspaces" (403).

time-space compression such as Enlightenment, Modernism, and Post-modernism.) Secondly, subjects are exposed to these mechanisms and their responses are shaped by them. As I will show later, Harvey is critical of such Foucauldian totalizations; however, he accepts the Lefebvrian dimensions of social space. He does not detach space from social relations either. He claims that "the ability to influence the production of space is an important means to augment social power," which involves the enforcement of "influence over the ways of representing space, as well as over space of representation" (233).

Space is thus a social product, as well as a "political and economic phenomenon" (255) in the service of an abstract politics that, in Harvey's understanding, is often concretized in space through economic changes. (Spatial) change, for example, due to economic investments, indicates simultaneously "a reorganization of the framework through which social power is expressed" (255). In this sense, spatial change serves the maintenance of some status quo. Harvey is straightforward about this: "the accumulation of capital is perpetually deconstructing that social power by reshaping its geographical bases. Put the other way round, any struggle to reconstitute power relations is a struggle to reorganize their spatial bases" (238). Power, space, and place are interrelated categories that are responsible for channeling social relations. Harvey conceptualizes thereby macro-level politics as well as the micro politics of place or, as Soja also claims, the "microspaces of power" (*Postmodern Geographies* 24). The framework seems a dialectical constant of spatial dynamics for Harvey: "those who command space always control the politics of place even though [. . .] it takes control of some place to command space in the first instance" (234). Such dynamics based on space-place oppositionality has a unifying quality. Spatial change does not aim at diversification of the spatial paradigm, but at the "homogenization of space [. . .] that renders place subservient to transformations of space" (257). Place appears frozen in the politico-spatial matrix,[10] just as the system of production creates spatial fixes (see *The New Imperialism*).

Time-space compressions appear as socio-spatial dialectic in Soja's theorizing. Drawing heavily on Foucault and Lefebvre, he also insists that spatiality is a social product (*Postmodern Geographies* 129); more concretely, "the organization, and meaning of space is a product of social translation, transformation, and experience" (79-80). Space, in his interpretation, does not

---

[10] Such fixation intensifies the oppression of the subject, however places in Harvey's judgment appear to be minimal units that grant protection for people as well as they can be taken as the birthplace of opposition in the grand scheme of this "absolute antagonism" (257): spaces "form a fixed frame within which the dynamics of a social process must unfold. [. . .] The effect is to unleash capitalism's powers of 'creative destruction' upon the geographical landscape, sparking violent movements of opposition from all kinds of quarters" (258).

embody an individual creation either, even though he speaks of three spaces, the physical, mental, and social that "interrelate and overlap" (120). In this sense, the individual is positioned in space, and does not invent it; or rather, as Soja claims, "spatiality is simultaneously the medium and outcome [. . .] of social action and relationship" (129). Quite straightforwardly, Soja places the human subject in a network of social relations called space, whereby he comes close to "an instrumental cartography of power and social control" (63), as he puts it regarding Frederick Jameson; and also to Foucault, who claims that "power relations are rooted in the system of social networks" ("The Subject and Power" 224).

Accordingly, Soja conceptualizes with his socio-spatial dialectic the production and reproduction of social relations. He thus proposes that social relations are spatially organized as "social life [is] both space-forming and space contingent" (*Postmodern Geographies* 129), thereby arguing for an interdependence between space and social relations; as well as for spatiality that does not correspond to stability. By claiming that social relations are space contingent, Soja also proposes that space and time are interrelated as social change, transformation, or "contradiction and struggle" (129) take place also in space. As he claims explicitly, "the spatiality of social life is rooted in temporal/historical contingency" (130). So when Soja speaks about "dominant centres," "subordinate peripheries," and "socially created and polarized spatial relations" (78)—about spatialized hierarchical power structures (the way organized space appears to be constituted through)—he conceptualizes such a structure not as a "once-for-all event" (129). Instead, it seems that temporal/historical contingency means for him both "dependence" and "occurrence" and thus spatiality is constantly reproduced out of a socio-spatial-temporal pulp.[11]

Post-Marxist propositions clearly present the defocalization of the subject and the focus on politicized space. Space falls prey to power discourses and becomes transformed in their likeness. The technology of space produces space so that it serves as a tool or as the arch dispositif to channel power mechanisms. Hence space appears as the interstitial entity that serves as an important part in the realization of the power establishment and, consequently, in the indoctrination of the subject. However, space as product cannot be seen as stable in the sense that it would be unchanging; exactly because of its product quality in the function of the socio-political framework, it follows the transformations of the power matrix. Alone on this basis, planned fixity of both space and subject appears not only grave but also limited; yet, as I will show subsequently, these

---

[11] However, the struggle over production and reproduction Soja's "spatial matrix" (129) indicates is not a democratic coercion, but, in the first place, it marks the struggle of the power structure to maintain the existing order. Much in Louis Althusser's sense, then, struggle can be seen as overdetermined.

propositions, as in the case of phenomenologists and humanist geographers, gain integrity along with the softening features of their theory. It is as much as to say that post-Marxist thinkers too grant the subject a pool of action in this rigid grid.

2.3. Hybridizing Space and Place: The In-between

Despite the circumstance that the foregoing propositions are pessimistic many times over, they do not disallow the possibility of at least a degree of human freedom, most often in the form of struggle. Just as phenomenologists cannot and do not want to exclude factors that effect the conceptualization of the subject in a broader matrix than merely the subject, post-Marxists also call for a more integrated spatial framework. Let us turn now to this coercive spatial framework of production and construction.

Foucault, for example, insisting on a method examining forms of power, proposes to investigate realms of resistance directly, as the oppositional character of these spaces sheds light on the nature of power structure. At the same time, however, spaces of resistance enhance fissures in absolute space, establishing antidiscourses within it:

> if it is true that at the heart of power relations and as a permanent condition of their existence there is an insubordination and a certain essential obstinacy on the part of the principles of freedom, then there is no relationship of power without the means of escape or possible flight. Every power relationship implies, at least *in potentia,* a strategy of struggle [. . .]. ("The Subject and Power" 225)

This notion can be detected all across the critical discourse, starting with Heidegger, who claims that "*Raum* means a place cleared or freed for settlement and lodging. A space is something that has been made room for, something that is cleared and free, namely within a boundary. [. . .] *Accordingly, spaces receive their being from locations and not from 'space'*" ("Building" 154). Heidegger's distinction between space and place in this section does not pertain to the politics of space; however, the enabling character of place in contrast to space is revealing. In fact, this aspect has been polarized into the fissure in abstract space through which pluralism, despite superimposed homogeneity, can be obtained. Thus, Lefebvre conceptualizes difference to the spite of homogeneity (372):

> Differences endure or arise on the margins of the homogeneous realm, either in the form of resistances or in the form of externalities (lateral, heterotopical, heterological). What is different is, to begin with, what is *excluded*: the edges of the city, shanty towns, the spaces of forbidden games, of guerrilla war, of war. Sooner or later, however, the existing

center and the forces of homogenization must seek to absorb all such differences, and they will succeed if these retain a defensive posture and no counterattack is mounted on their side. (373)

Heterotopical space deconstructs the homogeneous notion of abstract space. Through the juxtaposition of different spaces Foucault argues for a heterogeneous space in which the different spatialities do not exist in hierarchy: "we live inside a set of relations that delineates sites which are irreducible to one another and absolutely not superimposable on one another" ("Of Other Spaces" 23). Spatialities can thus coexist, but they are interrelated as well as they oppose each other (24). This suggests a pluralist, even democratic, spatial understanding as abstract space becomes not only fragmented, but also defocalized and decentralized, even though the different spaces tighten against each other. It must also be mentioned that these "singular spaces [are] to be found in some given social spaces" ("Space, Power and Knowledge" 168). Social—abstract or transparent—space, then, is yet apparent, not necessarily as a physical grid of a built environment, but one that is present through, for example, its dispositifs.

Foucault mentions two kinds of heterogeneous spaces. One is unreal space or utopia "with no real place" ("Of Other Spaces" 24), and the other type is represented by heterotopias. Heterotopias do not only depict a pluralist notion of space through their otherness, but they can also be parts of abstract space. For example, "crisis heterotopias" or "heterotopias of deviation," which are mentioned by Foucault directly, can indeed be seen as dispositifs to enforce the existing power structure. As Foucault claims, it is society that makes each heterotopia function with "a precise and determined function" (25). However, what is striking from the point of view of the present inquiry is that, by Foucault's definition, heterotopias refer to places that are "simultaneously represented, contested, and inverted" (24), and that they are "capable of juxtaposing in a single real place several spaces, several sites that are in themselves incompatible" (25). Heterotopias represent inherent building blocks in society; but, furthermore, the notions of contestation, inversion, as well as their otherness despite the spatial context can render them places of resistance. Thus when Foucault explains that "[heterotopias] have a function in relation to all the space that remains" (27), the "relation" may well be that of opposition, and not only "illusion" or "compensation" (both functions support society's image of itself) (27).

In addition, the inner structure of heterotopias reveals a great deal about the nature of places of otherness. The juxtaposition of different spaces in a single place has several implications. If, for example, several spaces have relation to the particular place, this place becomes apparently a part of these spaces at the same time, which questions the authenticity of the respective relation. Furthermore, if in such a place of resistance properties of abstract space can also be found, this place cannot be elsewhere in the sense that it refuses every tie to and every entity of abstract space; but, rather, it inverts them by redefining both ties and properties to suit its purposes. The presence of entities of abstract space may well mean the presence of abstract space itself, which holds the possibility of reorientation. In other words, as much as heterotopias can represent fissures in abstract space, in similar manner the presence of abstract space in heterotopias can disclose fissures in these heterotopias.

Yet the defocalization of abstract space remains a fact for Michel De Certau too. In his book *The Practice of Everyday Life* he conceptualizes the city as simulacrum, totalization, as well as a geometrical and theoretical construction (93) in contrast to daily practices that create a "*migrational*, or metaphorical city" (93). Using the metaphor of the "rhetoric of walking" (99) of the everyday pedestrian, he claims that "the long poem of walking manipulates spatial organizations, no matter how panoptic they may be" (101). Individual practice thus transcribes space much as Bourdieu or Casey sees it. De Certeau enframes this individual act in the "Concept-city" (95), which lures in the background of all activity of the subject, but it also provides the material to work with.

De Certeau's concept-city is described as technological, organized space in Foucault's, Harvey's, or Baudrillard's fashion, in which space and time, as well as the subject are reproduced according to "socioeconomic and political strategies" (95). Thus, as De Certeau explains, the city is "univocal" and "universal," "organized by 'speculative' and classificatory operations" (94), in which the subject is positioned in likewise manner. However, De Certeau inverts this scheme by adding that the concept-city is not transparent, for spatial practices destabilize the operational transparency of abstract space. Spatial practices, in fact, reinscribe space, that is, "secretly structure the determining conditions of social life" (96). What De Certeau does is to acknowledge abstract space as context, but what he denies is its totalizing and panoptic character by granting individual praxis the upper-hand in place-construction. This proposition renders his theory akin to Foucault's heterotopia in that individual spatial practice is juxtaposed with the praxis of other individuals—a particular dynamics that establishes a network of spatialities overlapping with abstract space.

Walking becomes similar to a speech act that creatively enhances the subject's intention in the geographical context. Through walking the subject appropriates the topography by establishing relations between places (97-98), much in the way Heidegger does with his de-distancing. As De Certeau has it, walking actualizes the spatial order as "the crossing, drifting away, or improvisation of walking privilege, transform or abandon spatial elements" (98). It alters time deposited in the spatial setting as well as individualizes it by way of selection. De Certeau understands these in the function of "the present, the discrete, the 'phatic'" (98). The latter calls attention to the social aspect of spatial reinscription whereby "phatic *topoi*" (99) express different modalities. The modalities of walking can be as diverse as the modalities of language; however, here I want to refer to the individuality of statements a particular walking route can express, and to the alterations it can effect regarding abstract space: "Walking affirms, suspects, tries out, transgresses, respects, etc., the trajectories it 'speaks'" (99).

Walking thus has the potential to contest and negate the space it moves in, creating actual heterotopias. Contestation and negation are achieved through storytelling, which creates an alternative space:

> For the technological system of a coherent and totalizing space that is 'linked' and simultaneous, the figure of pedestrian rhetoric substitute trajectories that have a mythical structure [. . .] a story jerry-built out of elements taken from common sayings, an allusive and fragmentary story whose gaps mesh with the social practices it symbolizes. (102)

Walking is asserted on the grounds of abstract space: it uses and manipulates the properties of abstract space. De Certeau uses here again figures of speech, especially synecdoche and asyndeton, that stylize the environment into "enlarged singularities and separate islands" (101). The story character of walking becomes extremely important in this discourse, since walking is not a purposeless moving about, but praxis that effects meaningful cohesion through history and causality. For De Certeau walking parallels individual language that communicates a message, and this message can be regarded as a proof of the subject's integrity. Furthermore, the story the subject's praxis establishes creates a space by the alteration of abstract space which coexists with both abstract space and the spaces established by similar praxis of other subjects.

In fact, the storytelling character of walking is the true source of heterotopias in De Certeau's theory. As people walk about in the city, they establish different stories that can give a different angle to things in the city, or complement each other. These stories, that is, spatialities, co-exist, overlap, or collide. No matter what, walking provides for "relationships and intersections [. . .] that intertwine and create an urban fabric" (103). In this sense, the city is not what we see: the grid, the technology, or the channeled history, for example; but, much rather, it becomes the text of subtexts inscribed by the praxis of subjects.

It must be mentioned, however, that De Certeau is also aware of the immense influence of the built environment on subjects. For example, names of streets as well as symbols (103) influence the perception of the walking route; they do not only establish a "magnetic field of trajectories" or "traffic patterns" (104), but also they have, in this way, a controlling function over the subject. In this sense, De Certeau yet maintains the policing character of the city and its panoptic gaze; conversely, this strand is also embedded in the appropriation context of what is believable, memorable, or primitive (he explains these as "legend," "memory," and "dream") (105). These aspects symbolize both the trigger and the result of the walking practice, echoing Bourdieu's and Casey's idea of the habitus. For De Certeau the city is inhabited with the help of this three stranded mechanism, since they enact "a crack in the system that saturates places with signification" (106).

The fissure in the dominant discourse has become *third space* in Homi Bhabha's theory: the heterotopia effected by the mobility engendered by walking can be regarded as third space. It is hybrid space that connects to the subject's habitus-driven activity. Furthermore, it reflects the subject's creative use of the spaces, in which s/he is embedded, and the transformation, or rather transcendence, of the grid of domineering discourses. As Bhabha establishes,

> The intervention of the Third Space of enunciation, which makes the structure of meaning and reference an ambivalent process, destroys this mirror of representation in which cultural knowledge is customarily revealed as integrated, open, expanding code. Such an intervention quite properly challenges our sense of the historical identity of culture as homogenizing, unifying force, authenticated by originary Past, kept alive in the national tradition of the People. (37)

Hybridization echoes the phenomenological use of space in that dwelling is to be understood as the focal point to which everything is rendered: "Spaces open up by the fact that they are let into the dwelling of man. To say that mortals *are* is to say that *in dwelling* they persist through spaces by virtue of their stay among things and locations. And only because mortals pervade, persist through, spaces by their very nature are they able to go through spaces" ("Building" 157). Heidegger acknowledges the existence of spatialities other than the subject's, even though they remain secondary, or veiled, and lost in the enculturating activity of the subject. Concomitantly, third space describes the hybrid movement of the subject that is not a simple negation of social space—a mere recentering of the subject. Much rather, it is "thirding-as-othering" (*Thirdspace* 60)[12], which is a tactics both negating and building upon the given socio-spatial paradigm.

There are two implications of such a spatial framework. First, in such a space coercion is an inbuilt check-in-balance for abstract space, which accounts

---

[12] Soja uses "thirding" much as Bhabha does. For him it represents "a critical 'other-than' choice that speaks and critiques through its otherness. That is to say, it does not derive simply from an additive combination of its binary antecedents but rather from a disordering, deconstruction, and tentative reconstitution of their presumed totalization producing an open alternative that is both similar and strikingly different" (61).

for the dynamics of space construction and production. Second, this spatial understanding does not produce a distilled and transparent framework. Conversely, boundaries of both abstract space and counterspaces cannot be held apart because of boundary crossing/transgression from both sides. Such mutual encroaching is, indeed, not only effected by way of heterotopous juxtaposition. One important method with which counterspaces are established is via hybridization of already existing spatial paradigms. Hybridization, in the light of the previous discussion, becomes realized by the deliberate praxis of subjects: through praxis, subjects establish third spaces reinscribing and restructuring space.[13] This results in a playfulness or mobility as such a tactics resists categorization or fixity, since it is beyond categorization from the point of view of social space.

---

[13] These spaces can mark reengendering race, gender, or ethnicity through the recreation of a usable past that also renders the present manageable (see, e.g., Gerald Vizenor, Gloria Anzaldúa, as well as Hurston).

3. Zora Neale Hurston: Cultural Space, and African American Spatiality

> We Negroes here are out in front of others because there is something inherent on this continent that springs. Hence a new ingredient was given to our African material that gave it life and the element to reach people and endure. I am perfectly reconciled to slavery on that score. It had to be, or other things could not have happened. ("To Jean Parker Waterbury" 645)

> But in the main, I feel like a brown bag of miscellany propped against a wall. Against a wall in company with other bags, white, red and yellow. Pour out the contents, and there is discovered a jumble of small things priceless and worthless. A first-water diamond, an empty spool, bits of broken glass, lengths of string, a key to a door long since crumbled away, a rusty knife-blade, old shoes saved for a road that never was and never will be, a nail bent under the weight of things too heavy for any nail, a dried flower or two still a little fragrant. In your hand is the brown bag. On the ground before you is the jumble it held—so much like the jumble in the bags, could they be emptied, that all might be dumped in a single heap and the bags refilled without altering the content of any greatly. A bit of colored glass more or less would not matter. Perhaps that is how the Great Stuffer of Bags filled them in the first place—who knows? ("How It Feels to Be Colored Me" 1655)

3.1. Hurston's Fiction as Cultural Space

Hurston resists categorization and places herself in the in-between; that is, she constructs her cultural space along very similar lines I have described as the "in-between" category above. Her approach does not represent a mere negation of social space, be it the social space of the white status quo or that of the Harlem intelligentsia. Much rather, she insists on revitalizing the given black cultural landscape by reemploying black tactics of cultural appropriation and contextualizing the African American subject in a remotivated cultural space.

Hurston scholarship places predominant emphasis on her use of language. Undoubtedly, the African American vernacular represents one significant element of her cultural space; moreover, language is a primary medium in negotiating and maintaining cultural links. As Stuart Hall maintains, "To belong to a culture is to belong to roughly the same conceptual and linguistic universe, to know how concepts and ideas translate into different languages, and how language can be interpreted to refer to or *reference* the world" ("Representation" 22). Furthermore, language is interwoven with all other notions of culture and, in this way, Hurston's (creative use of) language depicts African American cultural artifacts, texts, and, in general, of African American cultural space.

Hurston the anthropologist constructs her cultural framework based on the inclusion of African American rituals, mythology, and places—a practice that carries over into her fiction. What makes it all the more intriguing is that she also incorporates autobiographical material (see Hemenway). For instance, Eatonville (her hometown) takes a central position in the two novels—a town that plays an important role in her autobiography, *Dust Tracks on a Road*, as well as it is a subject of her ethnographic book, *The Florida Negro*. In fact, there are striking parallels between these books and the two novels. Consequently, her novels can be seen as the fictional realization of an anthropologically unique and deeply personal cultural space.

Hurston becomes the participant observer of her own cultural space, which influences her writing strategy. The use of the "spy-glass of Anthropology" (3) in her ethnographic[14] *Mules and Men*, crystallizes as a literary approach in her fictional works. The anthropological spy-glass enables her to gain insight into a community by becoming a member, while, simultaneously, maintaining the critical distance necessary for research. The insider/outsider dichotomy suggests, what Hall calls in another context, an "oppositional code" ("Encoding, Decoding" 102),[15] which, in fact, is characteristic of African American communication: "The theory behind our tactics: 'The white man is always trying to know into somebody else's business. All right, I'll set something outside the door of my mind for him to play with and handle. He can read my writing but he sho' can't read my mind. I'll put this play toy in his hand, and he will seize it and go away. Then I'll say my say and sing my song'" (*Mules and Men* 4-5). Hurston claims to possess the insider's view in the African American community: thus she professes authenticity for her research, and the reader can anticipate inside information s/he cannot get otherwise.

Hurston employs the anthropologist's strategy in her novels too, rendering them—to borrow Gábor Tamás Molnár's observation regarding anecdotes— "*more real, yet not less fictional, than analytic experiments of thought*" (45).[16] "Reconciling the subjective and the objective nature of her folkloric collection" (Hoffman-Jeep par. 13) is thus transposed as a writing strategy into her novels. Her narrators are the anthropologist-medium itself rendering the cultural text accessible for the reader. This can become observable in a manner not at all objective as the narrator may renegotiate its positioning to the text—in Geertzian *thick description*: the narrator's view becomes "unscientific" for

---

[14] I use the terms "anthropology" and "ethnography" interchangeably here, while ethnography is often considered the "general methodological framework" (Kedia and Van Willigen 13) of anthropology, that is, a method of a discipline. In Hurston's time the term anthropology was widely used, also pertaining to, what is referred to nowadays as, ethnography or cultural anthropology.

[15] Stuart Hall suggests a political strategy of interpretation, whereby the subject "detotalizes the message in the preferred code in order to retotalize the message in some alternative framework of reference" ("Encoding, Decoding" 102).

[16] All translations from Hungarian and German are mine.

articulating subjective opinions. One of the many examples in *Their Eyes* is the often ironic voice of the narrator passing value judgments on its subjects: evaluating Janie's *talking back* (to refer to bell hooks's way of feminine reassertion of the self), the narrator pityingly describes the masculine crowd surrounding Starks—her second husband—envying and despising him simultaneously, as "good-for-nothing's" (75) and "raggedy-behind squirts of sixteen and seventeen" (76). Similarly, the narrator in *Jonah's* relies on children's descriptions of Minnie Turl during the hide-and-seek game when identifying the young girl as "bow-legged" and "pigeon-toed" (21). *Their Eyes* can be regarded as a storytelling event,[17] in which the reader becomes a participant through the spyglass of the narrator; and *Jonah's*, from another point of view, is but a journey across the South, arcing over places "[. . .] a more porous array of intersections where distinct processes crisscross from within and beyond [that is, culture's] borders" (Rosaldo 495).[18] Through the assemblage of cultural events the two novels become, as does literary anthropology for Molnár, "simultaneously a model of reality for reality" (47).

Blending culture with fiction does not characterize Hurston's fiction only. In fact, merging culture and fiction has become a relevant focus of literary research:

> the relation of literature and anthropology prepares a humanities model in which the text produced by humans enables the understanding of culture, that is, cultural "facts" will all the more be accessible during the work with the text in the form of allegories. [. . .] The means and, at the same time, medium of this is the text. In our case anthropology is a paradigm constituted in and by the text. (Biczó and Kiss 9)

---

[17] Storytelling is an element in the African American cultural pantheon and has features that render it of interest for the cultural investigator. Walter J. Ong reveals in his seminal *Orality and Literacy* that in oral cultures people are more "communal and externalized" (68) as well as they rely on "fixed, formulaic thought patterns" (23) and "verbatim repetition" (57) in telling and remembering stories. Members of oral cultures are thus more attached to their groups, and their cultural performance, e.g., storytelling, is also of communal nature. Furthermore, storytelling characterizes the cultural setting in which it appears for the recurrence of cultural elements (topics, phrases, places, etc.) including "paralinguistic features along with body movements" (Champion 3) during the storytelling event, so it is culturally descriptive and can well serve the purposes of cultural revitalization (see Champion, Levine, and Smitherman).

[18] The postmodern anthropologist, Renato Rosaldo defines culture, rituals, and the positioning of the ethnographer in relation to his/her research subject—in this case the Ilongot headhunters. As in the quote, he questions the homogenous concept of culture by diversifying it, but he also recognizes his own situatedness, which renders his inquiry partial and subjective.

The function of literature as medium in the literature/anthropology equation is also emphasized by Mario Cesareo, who claims that "anthropology does not *encounter* literature [. . .]: it is engendered by it" (162). Even though Cesareo criticizes the, for him, sometimes forced relationship between anthropology and literature, he does acknowledge the relevance of ethnographic texts: "The determining element that makes a text ethnographic is the particular articulation of those rituals and practices with meaning and social structure" (161). Cesareo's argument also reveals that just as culture is (an assemblage of) text (see Clifford Geertz's *The Interpretation of Cultures*), text is also culture. As such, "[literary texts] exhibit how symbols are linked up with action and situations richly laden with conflict, how, beyond the weapon of the word and the power of images, they can simultaneously be functionalized for societal and political interests, as well as for ethnic self-presentation" (Bachmann-Medick 17). Doris Bachmann-Medick's account of the anthropological turn in literature ("anthropologische Wende"), diverting attention away from language-oriented inquiry toward cultural investigations, urges the conceptualization of literary texts as media "that already contain in themselves condensed forms of ethnographic description and interpretation of culture" (25). The anthropological hide-and-seek African American children play in *Jonah's* exemplifies Bachmann-Medick's statement. The children's game shows how they adopt it on a formal plantation in a Georgia setting with the narrator reporting about its formal aspects including the ditties chanted; but it stages the socialization of children into (gender) roles as well as, from a literary point of view, foreshadows the nature and, to some extent, structure of the conflicts evolving.

The cultural approach to literature emphasizes the multiplicity of reading, denying an objective interpretation: "Literature becomes both a creation and creator of culture, with anthropology as observer/reader/interpreter. The dual role for literature and the repositioning of anthropology allows for a multiplicity of possibilities in reading, writing about, and interpreting people, places, and perspectives, real or imagined" (De Angelis 2). Hurston represents a case in point: as a writer/anthropologist she practices both literature and anthropology at the same time; and she does this as a subjective insider.

From a cultural point of view, Hurston's cultural politics of insiderness in her fiction serves purposes of authentication. Janet Tallman's interpretation of the ethnographic novel reinforces Hurstonian approach to fiction:

> The ethnographic novel written by someone from within the culture has a point of view unsullied by the culture-boundness and the blind-spots that accompany any outsider, no matter how well-trained. Of course, the insider still has a biased point of view, influenced by class, gender, age,

and whatever other social categories are operative. Yet the insider novelist can have an authenticity, a knowledge of the culture, impossible for the anthropologist. (11)

Hurston's fiction models cultural rituals and processes in African American communities, and, thus, it can be seen as a series of anthropological treatises. Her ethnographic novels enact African American dramas depicting "personalised worlds of becoming, rather than static worlds of being" (James 4) as, thereby, she often recounts her field experiences.

Writing from within is a key position Hurston takes, both as a student of African American culture and as an African American subject; and she, then, goes further than writing simply fiction: by insisting on the spyglass of anthropology Hurston, the artist, offers ethnographic texts.

3.2. Hurston's African American Spatiality

As it has already been mentioned, Hurston research generally emphasizes her linguistic preoccupation. However, Hurston's employment of vernacular language is anchored in an awareness of African American culture and cultural dynamics, including African American spatial thinking. Examining the works of some of the most relevant contributors to the Hurston scholarship, one can see that the conceptualization of the vernacular or of African American literature purports a perhaps even more prevalent trait of her work: embeddedness in African American cultural space.

In *The Signifying Monkey: A Theory of African-American Literary Criticism*, Henry Louis Gates, Jr., uses the "Signifying Monkey" to refer to creative African American language use that he traces back to African traditions. Deliberately, Gates connects it to tricksterism that, as demonstrated in the subsequent analyses, is one of Hurston's important observations regarding African American culture. For Gates the "Signifying Monkey" represents "the figure-of-figures, [. . .] the trope in which are encoded several other peculiarly black rhetorical tropes"; and, from the point of view of African American literary tradition, "a metaphor for formal revision, or intertextuality, within the Afro-American literary tradition" (xxi). Gates identifies several modes of signifying (e.g., tropological revision, the speakerly text, talking texts, and rewriting the speakerly), all of them connected to other texts, creating an African American literary tradition.

Gates places Hurston in a tradition of quest for a literary voice, which he exemplifies with Hurston's recuperating to Frederick Douglass's use of the ship metaphor (the opening metaphor of *Their Eyes*). Gates demonstrates that Hurston's reworking of the metaphor is in fact an African American strategy of revision, which pointedly places her in a tradition of "relational signification"

(Siemerling 39). In the line of this investigation, it is indeed one of the points that reveals Hurston's cultural preoccupation: in a quest for voice, Hurston uses a rhetorical strategy, which in cultural terms is a trickster strategy, to be understood in the function of chiasmus (Gates 172)—standing in the crossroads, Hurston employs a style, both a continuum of African American tradition and a linkage to established literary traditions, representing a merger of and a constant shift between the two paradigms. As Gates puts it, "Hurston's very rhetorical strategy [. . .] seems designed to mediate between [. . .] a profoundly lyrical, densely metaphorical, quasi-musical, privileged black oral tradition on the one hand, and a received but not yet fully appropriated standard English literary tradition on the other hand" (174). Hurston's "speakerly text" (174) based on "free indirect discourse" (xxv) is "to represent an oral literary tradition" (181). In-betweenness and dynamic rhetorical movement refer not only to the becoming African American subject in *Their Eyes*—they "reflect a certain development of self-consciousness in a hybrid character, a character who is neither the novel's protagonist nor the text's disembodied narrator, but a blend of both, an emergent and merging moment of consciousness" (xxv-xxvi)—but, in my view, also to African American cultural understanding of a hybrid subject embedded in a cultural context. As I will show subsequently, Janie's act of storytelling in her backyard proves ingraining in both community and literary tradition, as well as the tangible advent of the female subject in a hybrid way— of which the location of the backyard is a clear indication.

Hurston's cultural space goes beyond reification of African American language use to enhance an (emerging) African American (literary) tradition:

> The narrative voice Hurston created, and her legacy to Afro-American fiction, is a lyrical and disembodied yet individual voice, from which emerges a singular longing and utterance, a transcendent, ultimately racial self, extending far beyond the merely individual. Hurston realized a resonant and authentic narrative voice that echoes and aspires to the status of the impersonality, anonymity, and authority of the black vernacular tradition, a nameless, selfless tradition, at once collective and compelling, true somehow to the unwritten text of a common blackness. For Hurston, the search for a telling form of language, indeed the search for a black literary language itself, defines the search for the self. (183)

More important than pinpointing the relevance of the black vernacular, Gates, not at all unwillingly, calls attention to characteristics of African Americanness and to Hurston's cultural insiderness. Clear as it is, Hurston's "intra-communal intertextuality" (Siemerling 44) manifests the creative, yet harmonious tension between communality and individualism along with a quest for voice, literary or otherwise.

The intracommunal aspect in Hurston's works can be approached on the basis of a blues pattern as blues proves an African American cultural archetype for her: both Janie and Tea Cake in *Their Eyes* are blues performers and blues itself is a connector between people in the muck. Houston A. Baker's vernacular theory explicated in *Blues, Ideology, and Afro-American Literature: A Vernacular Theory* depicts the relevance of blues as a cultural performance. Baker argues for an "ancestral matrix" deriving from the "material conditions of slavery" and blues (2). Blues represents for him "a phylogenetic recapitulation—a nonlinear, freely associative, nonsequential meditation—of species experience [and] an anonymous (nameless) voice issuing from the black (w)hole" (5). His insistence on a cultural tradition and identity is rather similar to that of Gates's—his dynamic notion of Signifyin(g) regarding the binary of the communal and the individual. For Baker blues is "always becoming, shaping, transforming, displacing the peculiar experiences" (5) and it is an individual act. Yet, blues appears in his theorizing as "a code radically conditioning Afro-American signifying" (5). The blues as code also sets the frame for interpretation of the particular piece and that in relation to other pieces: "the blues [. . .] comprise a meditational site where familiar antinomies are resolved (or dissolved) in the office of adequate cultural understanding" (6).

The underlying notion of blues is, then, an understanding based on cultural performativity. It envisions a communicational framework in relation to which subjects seek to express themselves. Blues is thus the anthropological rather than a linguistic means of encrypting and decrypting. As Winfried Siemerling reminds us,

> Baker's blues matrix, however, suggests also a discursive orchestration that draws particular attention to the performative aspect of representation itself. [. . .] [D]espite his insistence on the vernacular, Baker draws our attention to the specific performative aspect of the representation of culture, which constantly helps to *create* new cultural references and social constellations as it responds to previous ones. (56-57)

It is in the function of a blues matrix that Janie's "expressiveness" (59) renders her a "storyteller and blues singer par excellence" (59) in *Their Eyes*, for she "recapitulates the blues experience of all black women treated as 'mules of the world'" (58). The attentive reader can see that the nature of blues is a permanent shift between individual and community in a cultural dialogue, where the individual relates to the blues framework and the latter is also constantly reshaped by individual performance.

At the same time, the trickster quality of blues performance suggests that the trickster is not only an inherent cultural recuperation, as Gates has it in his chapter dealing with the Yoruba trickster, Esu Legba; but also a political act in the production matrix of a power framework:

> Fixity is a function of power. Those who maintain place, who decide what takes place and dictate what has taken place, are power brokers of the traditional. The "placeless," by contrast, are translators of the nontraditional. Rather than fixed in the order of cunning Grecian urns, their lineage is fluid, nomadic, transitional. Their appropriate mark is a crossing sign at the junction.
>
> The crossing sign is the antithesis of a place marker. It signifies, always, change, motion, transience, process. (Baker 202)

Blues performers, as cultural nomads, do not merely claim voice in a cultural space, but also perform political acts in opposition to power structures. Both Hurston's protagonists, Janie in *Their Eyes* and John in *Jonah's*, move between places and appear placeless for the time being. Yet, their acquired/reclaimed mobility expresses in-betweeness in the political matrix of social space. As I will argue later, elsewhereness, besides denoting strengthening of the African American cultural core, manifests an oppositional political statement. Emphasis is placed on oppositionality in contrast to which action is undertaken as a centripetal act of selfassertion.

It is important to point out that Hurston is conscious about the relevance of vernacular. When exploring African American contribution to American culture—features of African American (folk) art in her "Characteristics," she acknowledges the linguistic contribution under the headings "Dialect" and "Will to Adorn," by which she means African American tendency of ornamenting speech and reinterpreting already given words and phrases through metaphors and similes, double descriptives, as well as verbal nouns (50-52).

As a matter of fact, Hurston discusses outspokenly the performative and intracommunal nature of African American language and culture, as well as the essentially spatial understanding of the African American subject. She identifies African American performatism as drama. It is the underlying principle of both language and action. As she claims, "Every phase of Negro life is highly dramatized. [. . .] Everything is acted out" (49). Acting out has a twofold dimension. It has a clearly linguistic aspect as "[African American] words are action words." However, she also suggests that action accompanies or precedes speech:

> The primitive man exchanges descriptive words. His terms are all close fitting. Frequently the Negro, even with detached words in his

vocabulary—not evolved in him but transplanted on his tongue by contact—must add action to it to make it do. [. . .] [T]he speaker has in his mind the picture of the object in use. Action. Everything is illustrated. So we can say that the white man thinks in a written language and the Negro thinks in hieroglyphics. (49-50)

Language is not merely a direct borrowing, or the vehicle of African American thought, but it is intertwined with dramatization/spatialization through action.

On the basis of Hurston's explication of African American culture, one can easily expect a heavy emphasis on the visual basis of expression in her cultural space. An aspect of it is body talk—yet another manifestation of African American drama. Body movements, as hieroglyphics themselves, have for Hurston a communicative value: they form a part of African American signifying. The young girl, Daisy, for instance, "is walking a drum tune" in *Their Eyes*:

> You can almost hear it by looking at the way she walks. She is black and she knows that white clothes look good on her. So she wears them for dress up. She's got those big black eyes with plenty shiny white in them that makes them shine like brand new money and she knows what God gave women eyelashes for, too. Her hair is not what you might call straight. It is negro hair, but it's got a kind of white flavor. Like the piece of string out of a ham. It's not ham at all, but it's been around ham and got the flavor. It was spread down thick and heavy over her shoulders and looked just right under a big white hat. (63-64)

Her movements denote specific meanings in an individual way; furthermore, they have a communal aspect: they appear always in a context in relation to other actors. In this case she is being watched by the men on the porch and they start an "acting-out courtship" (63), during which "the boys ha[ve] to act out their rivalry too" (64). Beyond concerting masculine action for and against Daisy, what renders this scene ultimately communal is the response of the audience: "the porch enjoyed the play and helped out whenever extras were needed" (64). In this way, the individual action of Daisy, the men, and members of the audience blends into communal space. In reality such dramas enacted in body movements emerge in a sequence between several actors as a call-and-response pattern traditional in African American culture. In "Characteristics" Hurston ascribes importance to dancing exactly on this ground. For her "Negro dancing is dynamic suggestion" and "compelling insinuation" (55)—dancing (body movement) is discursive in the complex relation of communality and individuality.

From the point of view of spatial analysis, what Hurston highlights in her essay is the inherently spatial thinking of African Americans, and what she describes is African American appropriation of space. Regarding her understanding of African American cultural space, she mentions specific organizing principles that help unfold African American spatial settings.

She identifies African Americans' preoccupation "to avoid the simple straight line" (54) when they furnish their homes. "Angularity" suggests that African Americans always find a way to adopt space to express the African American self, whether influenced by worldview or a desire to break away from the politico-spatial setting in the particular time-space compression. "Asymmetry" is a similar organizing principle, even if it pertains, in the first place, to the paradoxical juxtaposition of rhythm and the absence of symmetry (55) in African American art. For Hurston, these principles have special significance as they refer to African American tactics of cultural appropriation, as well as adaptation to diverse circumstances.

The acknowledgment of, and the preoccupation with different cultural elements have been constant in African American thought. Elaborating on the nature of African American religion, W.E.B. DuBois identified "three things [that] characterized this religion of the slave,—the Preacher, the Music, and the Frenzy" (116). DuBois's essential African Americanisms are in exact line with Hurston's observations regarding African American culture. Similarly to Hurston, DuBois accentuates the visual/spatial orientation in African American culture, whereby dramas enacted by the body, music expressing inherent and original Africanness, as well as culture heroes, which are not only cultural, but also structural categories, become primary carriers of culture. DuBois's preacher can be taken as a culture hero in Hurstonian conceptualization. DuBois defines him as "a leader, a politician, an orator, a 'boss,' an intriguer, an idealist,—all these he is, and ever, too, the centre of a group of men" (116). This characterization renders the preacher a structural force in the community with trickster qualities. More recent studies problematize the essence of African American culture in a similar manner (see Michael L. Hecht et al.). Defocalizing the primacy of the vernacular, Jack L. Daniel and Geneva Smitherman argue that "callresponse spans the sacred-secular continuum in Black Culture" (27). They posit that call-and-response does not only describe a communicational strategy in the African American community, but it also recuperates a worldview inherent in African Americans. The essentially Africanist notion situates the African American subject in a collectivist as well as contextualizing framework: call-and-response depicts the symbiotic joint movement of individuals with each other and with nature. In this way, it follows "natural rhythms" (32) or "interdependent rhythms" (34), and requires "community participation" (33). On a more abstract level, call-and-response denotes embedded interaction, which does not follow a simple pattern: "Harmony in nature and the universe is provided by the complementary, interdependent, synergic interaction between the spiritual and the material" (34).

From a closer look, Hurston's concepts of angularity, asymmetry, and drama precipitate the very same ideas. Her view of African American culture places the African American subject in an intact cultural/cosmological framework that can be called harmonious for its stability and unity. However, inherent are pluralism and heteronomy in this cultural framework also, as these notions provide its dynamics. Thus tension is natural, while belongingness remains an axiom. As the seeming controversy between individual and group in African American community proves conspicuous, a binary becomes obvious in Hurston's ethnographic writing and in her imagined communities as well. As Daniel and Smitherman argue *vis-à-vis* African American communication dynamics:

> The individual is challenged to do what he can within the traditional mold, and he is reaffirmed by the infinite possibilities for unique responses. Centuries-old group norms are balanced by individualized, improvisational emphases. By taking advantage of process, movement, creativity of the moment, and emotional, intuitive, and spiritual guidance, the individual can exercise his sense of Self by virtue of his unique contribution to the Group. (35)

In a constant back-and-forth vibration, the individual (or writer) emerges as a member of the community, constantly reifying identity in dialogic sequences regarding others all "in a unified movement" (34). John's last preaching in *Jonah's* offers a case in point. It follows the structure of African American sermons, that is, it evolves around rhetorical peaks in the process of bearing up. John thereby calls on traditional African American rhetorical elements— addressing the congregation, repetitions with increasing impetus, and familiar images—which resonate familiarly in his audience; while he finishes the cultural/rhetorical patterns in an individual way: "It [that is, the psalm sung] wakes up a whole family uh thoughts, and Ahm gointer speak tuh yuh outa de fullness uh mah heart" (174).

The interdependence of individual and group is a basic feature which undergirds Hurston's multidimensional approach to African American culture and determines her writing style. Furthermore, her emphasis on the performative nature of African American culture, whereby individual contribution may appear as a dissent from the group, refers to centripetality in the function of interdependence. Ultimately, the apparent outsiderness of Hurston's protagonists—just like Hurston's own in the Harlem Renaissance—reveals only the surface structure of their (thus her) universe. In reality, dissent is just another form of performative action, showing individual striving to strengthen the core of the African American community.

Unforeseen and unprescribed individual response enhances improvisation while remaining in the cultural framework (as it is, in an initiation ritual the whole sequence of the ritual counts, that is, the candidate's exclusion from the community as well as his/her placement in the in-between is transitionary, and s/he finally emerges as a member of the community). Improvisational response is facilitated for Hurston by tricksterism, a core element in African American culture. Tricksters and trickster qualities are not unknown phenomena in African Americans folk thought (see Roberts) and for Hurston, a researcher of folk culture, they are within her ken. She directly addresses this issue in *Sanctified*— e.g., regarding culture heroes such as Big John de Conqueror—and her other ethnographic books, but also her folktale collection, *Every Tongue Got to Confess: Negro Folk-tales from the Gulf States* offers ample examples. As it comes to expression through cultural tricksters, African American culture is an integrated whole, independent despite multi-layer embeddedness in overlapping cultural contexts: "Tricksters and trickster energy articulate a whole other, independent, cultural reality and positive way of negotiating multiple cultural systems" (Ammons xi). Such an approach to culture reifies selfaffirmation, a notion that carries special significance for a writer like Hurston in the racial climate of the Harlem Renaissance.

Hurston's cultural/textual space is endowed with a similar, trickster dynamics that she consciously plays down. The dynamic character of her space bears similarity to trickster strategies; as Deborah G. Plant asserts, these strategies form "patterns of behavior recognizable in Hurston's life and work— silence, shamming, tomming, signifying, masking, and posturing—[that] are all patterns of behavior exhibited in archetypal African American trickster figures" (45). As the subsequent chapters will demonstrate, both Janie's and John's journeys depict trickster energies, since their constant jumping in and out of roles reveals multifacial identities which are shaped by the demands of the situation. Multiplicity can be pinpointed in Janie's behavior in particular: from the point of view of the (patriarchal) community, her transgressive conduct that leads her to violate the norms of marriage as a patriarchal institution, her rebellious insistence on joining games not meant for her—e.g., shooting and playing the checkers—as well as her cross-dressing at the end of her story, but, perhaps, most strikingly her engagement in a storytelling activity show oscillation between worlds and a refusal of fixity. The trickster approach lends Hurston's fictional works a hybrid character and, as a result, Janie is able to transform her environment and her home. Her constant hybridizing—or thirding—builds on given cultural schemes such as African American places and tactics of identity negotiation.

African American places and identity negotiation closely relate to each other. Geographically speaking, one can say that spatial thinking denotes a matrix of here and there; however, from another point of view, it signifies boundary-making, that is, space is a vehicle of definition. In this respect, space is a category representing both difference and inclusion.

More specifically, African American geographical displacement enforced, what can be called, a horizontal spatial differentiation. In his book *From Behind the Veil: A Study of Afro-American Narrative*, Robert B. Stepto conceptualizes an African American spatial framework based on a North-South symbolic paradigm.[19] Discussing an "Afro-American pregeneric myth of the quest for freedom and literacy" (167), Stepto identifies two types of narratives: "ascent" and "immersion" narratives. These types represent two spatial orientations toward a "symbolic North" and a "symbolic South" respectively. In his coinage:

> The classic ascent narrative launches an "enslaved" and semiliterate figure on a ritualized journey to a symbolic North; that journey is charted through spatial expressions of social structure, invariably systems of signs that the questing figure must read in order to be both increasingly literate and increasingly free. The ascent narrative conventionally ends with the questing figure situated in the least oppressive social structure afforded by the world of the narrative, and free in the sense that he or she has gained sufficient literacy to assume the mantle of an articulate survivor. (167)

Freedom is constituted here as physical escape from racist environments, but, at the same time, the North-bound journey means also disruption of traditional communal ties (167). Conversely, ascent represents growing individualism including a growing sense of alienation in urban environments.

By contrast, immersion narratives have their focus on a "symbolic South"—denoting an oppositional movement, which represents recuperation to the African American community:

> the immersion narrative is fundamentally an expression of a ritualized journey into a symbolic South, in which the protagonist seeks those aspects of tribal literacy that ameliorate, if not obliterate, the conditions imposed by solitude. The conventional immersion narrative ends almost paradoxically, with the questing figure located in or near the narrative's

---

[19] A reworking of symbolic regions appears in Judylyn Ryan's dissertation, "Water from an Ancient Well: The Recuperation of Double-Consciousness." In an expansion of Stepto's theory of a symbolic North and South, Ryan establishes another binary, a "symbolic East" and a "symbolic West." The former is associated with an "imagined or literal" (Pavlíc xviii) African cultural core, while the latter accounts for "a foreign location of terror and bondage" (xviii).

most oppressive social structure but free in the sense that he has gained or regained sufficient tribal literacy to assume the mantle of an articulate kinsman. (167)

The relinking to a common African American past brings about a sense of freedom despite the retained oppressive racial climate. Community, as "balms of group identity" (6), plays an important role associated with the South.

The duality of North and South and the ambivalence associated with the antithetical, northward/southward movements embody the doubleness represented by DuBois, Gates, and Baker, as well as dramatized by Hurston—notably, both her protagonists in the two novels migrate South and find fulfillment there. The spatial dichotomy shows differing value systems associated with geographical regions embedded in the African American experience.

African American spatial thinking appears on a vertical level too. Edward M. Pavlíc identifies an "above-underground emergence" ("Syndetic Redemption" 165), whereby underground realms are conceptualized by him as "underground communal space," in which "people perform [. . .] aspects of their subjectivity which remain off limits, or abstracted, in secluded contemplation [and where] the diasporic modernist self becomes an accumulating repertoire of presences summoned from personal depth and communal interactions both past and present" (*Crossroads* 24). Underground spaces are formulated in opposition to above-ground spaces, but they signify terrains of authenticating cultural performances on individual as well as group level.

A similar concept of the underground is formulated in Baker's theorizing, proving inherent spatio-cultural thinking in African American expression. In his discussion of Richard Wright's *Black Boy*, Baker suggests the introduction of the term "black hole" to refer to "the subsurface force of the black underground" (151)—"the subterranean *hole* where the trickster has his ludic, deconstructive being" (151). The opposition between underground and aboveground spaces reifies African American situatedness in a socio-political structure, in which African Americans are forced to take a subservient position. The trope of the hole, which would indicate confinement and limitation, is, however, understood by Baker on the basis of the conceptualization of the black hole in physics as "an invisible, attractive force—a massive concentration of energy" (145). In this way, Baker turns it into a culturally-laden, positive category that goes beyond the underground/aboveground binary.

The hole, then, becomes a positive trope to depict African American "*Wholeness*, an achieved relationality of black community in which desire recollects experience and sends it forth as blues" (151). As I have demonstrated previously, the blues matrix is an essential performative tool of African American expression; however, Baker insists here on the physical and mental integrity of African Americans expressed in spatial terms. Blues performance in underground spaces is thus a means of escape, but it is the reaffirmation of the African American self too:

> To be *Black* and *(W)hole* is to escape incarcerating restraints of a white world (i.e., a *black hole*) and to engage the concentrated, underground singularity of experience that results in a blues desire's expressive fullness. [The black hole can be] conceived as a subcultural (underground, marginal, or liminal) region in which dominant, white culture's representations are squeezed to zero volume, producing a new expressive order. (151-2)

The reversal of spatial settings is thus African American culture's definite feature of tricksterism with a specific meaning: inversion marks appropriation of the environment to the self, and, as a result, it also proves the autonomy of the African American self. In Hurston's two novels underground performances in any of her inverted places—be it nonplace, sacred place, or feminine place—confirm subjectivity in place-making. The significance of underground spaces is that they do not refer to naturalization into the (white) socio-cultural setting,
but to the emergence as an African American subject in an African American cultural space, which, in Baker's line of thought, is the blues performance *par excellence*.

Both geographical strata, horizontal and vertical, prove undismissible in a study of Hurston's places. Regarding her own research of African American places described in her collection for the Federal Writers' Project, she gives account of mythical places of inversion that appear in African American folk thought. She was editor for the project in Florida in 1938-1939 (Hemenway 251), and her job also included collecting as well as writing (McDonogh xix). Her findings reflect features of the black underground. On the one hand, these places express, as Benjamin Albert Botkin asserts about places of the Old South, "the desire to return to a golden age" and are "closely related to the dream of a promised land" (469). On the other hand, this very feature reveals African American displacement and a response to it, rendering the experience of oppression meaningful after all. All four of Hurston's mythical places emphasize elsewhereness: *Diddy-Wah-Diddy* is a "way off somewhere" ("Negro Mythical Places" 107); *Zar* represents "the farthest point of the imagination" (108); *Beluthahatchee* is presented as "a land of forgiveness" (108); and *heaven* is conceptualized as a place irrecoverably out of reach (109). All of these places are seemingly detached from African American historical reality; however, they constitute important ways of selfevaluation as well as selfassertion. Similarly, the idea of *West Hell* stages another plastic expression of underground performance. It refers to the place of African American ritual of immersion.

During this wilderness experience, the culture hero with trickster qualities, Big John de Conqueror using his "wit, speed, and luck, as well as superb skill at fighting" (110) overcomes the devil. Trickster characteristics render this place also closely connected to underground performances.

In "Characteristics" Hurston emphasizes the role of real places also. In the first place, it is the jook, or pleasure house, that signifies an unique place in African American folk culture. It represents African American community in a microcosm (the muck in *Their Eyes* can, in fact, be taken as its idealized image). It is the place, where African American expression manifests itself with full force. Hurston acknowledges it as the birthplace of blues, and, in this way, it can be seen as the cradle of underground blues performance Baker accounts for, especially if the communal aspect of "incremental repetition" (63) in singing songs in the jook is taken into consideration. The jook provides thus the communal framework for individual conduct.

While Hurston's account of African American places in her ethnographic writings shows her spatial awareness, the meaning rendered to mythical places and other places (that I will deal with subsequently) indicate her keen interest in African American cultural performances. Her concern does not only pertain to ways of performance—tactics of insiderness, call-and-response, or tricksterism—but also to their location and context. In African American expression, spatial thinking often refers both to elsewhere in geographical terms, as geographical territories become imbued with certain culturally-informed meanings especially in opposition to other territories refashioned in the same way; and to an underground. The latter does not necessarily signify physical detachment, but much rather the reworking, that is, reterritorialization and reinscription of space.[20] The thirding of space and place appears seminal for Hurston as she encounters and integrates further African American places in her fiction. By making use of them, she consciously reworks and inverts them to establish hybrid places (for underground/trickster performances), thereby to construct her own cultural universe.

---

[20] There are many other relevant places that are inherent in the African American community: the plantation, as archetypal place of oppression; the city, the problematic image of African American modernity; or the train as the trope of fluidity as described in James Alan McPherson's *Railroad: Trains and Train People in American Culture*, among many others.

4. Black Cultural Space as Modernist Nonplace

4.1. Nonplace as a Means of Cultural Reassertion

Hurston's cultural space (both personal and fictional) displays characteristics of African American cultural performance. In fact, her rugged individualism and apparent antiestablishment attitude must be placed in this context: her cultural performance fits in an African American cultural matrix as described previously; that is, an apparently dissenting individual conduct in fact reasserts the African American cultural core. In examining Hurston's use of space and place as a source of her cultural politics, I will rely on the concepts of *nonplace* and *negative space*, useful concepts to shed light on Hurston's trickster politics in *Their Eyes Were Watching God* and *Jonah's Gourd Vine*.

Nonplaces come into view in postmodern geographies, representing fractured ties to architecture as buildings show a loss of anchorage in historical continuity. According to Marc Augé, nonplaces represent characteristic places of (super)modernity that are detached from historicity due to their nature as places of transition: they "cannot be defined as relational, or historical, or concerned with identity" (77-78). Although such places provide locales for social interaction, the type of interaction remains transitory and temporary. In a sense, these places cannot be claimed by any spatial paradigm, and they cannot be integrated into spatial stories of individuals. Concomitantly, they constitute a "world [. . .] surrendered to solitary individuality, to the fleeting, the temporary and ephemeral" (78) due to a kind of rootlessness in time and space. On the one hand, nonplace-like character derives exactly from the difference from the environment; on the other, difference is not at all surficial as nonplaces represent disruptions in the given spatial framework in both form and content.

From a different angle, though, certain actual places are similar to nonplaces in that they also appear as timeless, but are in fact prehistoric or ahistoric precipitations. Nancy D. Munn talks about negative space that is established through "spatial prohibition as a mode of boundary making" (93). She refers thereby to racist tactics of place-production. Australian Aborigines excluded from certain places are her examples; as well as negative spaces that are established by ritual. Thus whereas Augé's nonplaces are open to social activity, the latter kind of nonplaces are closed and not at all transient. These are ideological or sacred precipitations that are not to be trespassed. Yet their timelessness and asocial character connects them to Augé's nonplaces, an aspect that disallows them to become real places and that also excludes them from social interaction.[21]

---

[21] Munn's negative spaces can be described as "nowhereness" (Polk 7) and as "interstice" (xi). Nonplaces, however, can signify antipictures of places; that is, they can function as

What is striking is that nonplaces are not meaningless. Just as supermodern nonplaces can have an ideological function or can even be dispositifs in the mainstream spatial framework, Munn's negative spaces represent intact places. Aborigines' ritual of detour shows their awareness of these places, which they avoid constantly because they regard them as dangerous (94). As opposed to Augé's hyperreal nonplaces, Munn's negative spaces are integral in transparent social space, yet outside it.

Hurston's cultural space hybridizes both, seemingly mutually exclusive, aspects of nonplaces: their transience and their precipitation-like character. As a Modernist nonplace, her cultural universe can then be seen as hybridized space within the framework of Black Modernism. The reasons are twofold: first, criticized by the mainstream (and assimilationist) black intelligentsia—e.g., Langston Hughes and Richard Wright—Hurston's cultural space was regarded as unrealistic and inauthentic. In this sense, Hurston's space represents a marginal spatial discourse—a geopolitical aspect of nonplaces, that is, "With power generally understood to reside at the centre, [. . .] margins have usually been understood as simply objects of others' actions [and] comprehended as lacking subjectivity" (Browning and Joenniemi 700). Second, Hurston subverts her rendition and positioning as marginal by willfully realizing her space in opposition to white and black cultural space, while heavily embedding it in the latter. She inverts the Great Migration in her novels, redirecting it toward the South. In contrast to the North, the South holds for Hurston the mythic, hybridized cradle of African Americanness and as a means of criticism of Black Modernism.

For Hurston the South constitutes a black nonplace in contrast to the Modernist cultural space of the Harlem Renaissance. The sharp distinction is emphasized when the Great Migration is mentioned with irony in *Jonah's* as "dis Nawth bound fever lak eve'ywhere else" (149). Explicit irony reappears pronounced by the narrator, thereby rendering the statement all the more political: "On to the North! The land of promise" (151). There is an identifiable fissure within black cultural space, breaking it down into mainstream social space and distanced nonplace. *Jonah's* itself as "the antonym of discipline, order, rationality—the antithesis of 'civilized'" (Lemke 4) not only reifies

---

counterplaces to oppose mainstream power settings. In this way, they can have political content as far as they represent opposites, or even alternatives. As Nigel Rapport and Joanna Overing claim, "non-places serve the purpose of exploding the normative singularity of place; so that place and non-place represent contrastive modalities, the first never wholly" (293). Their definition further flavors Munn's understanding, but also Augé's, in that Rapport and Overing emphasize the contradictory relation between place and nonplace, while apparently suggesting that, as modalities, both are part of a larger social space.

superficially white conceptions about African Americans, but also embodies schism by standing in sharp contrast to the Harlem Renaissance's selfconception.

Apart from the geographical way of signifying, Hurston employs an antipicture of the Black Modernist ideology. The latter was influenced significantly by the drive of selfdefense against white depictions of African Americans, and as a result of which it converged toward white Modernism and centered around racial issues. W.E.B. DuBois articulates it precisely addressing the issue of African American double-consciousness in his *Souls of Black Folk*:

> [. . .] this sense of always looking at one's self through the eyes of the others, of measuring one's soul by the tape of a world that look on in amused contempt and pity. [. . .] The double aimed struggle of the black artisan–on the one hand to escape white contempt for a nation of mere hewers of wood and drawers of water, and on the other hand to plough and nail and dig for poverty-stricken horde–could only result in making him a poor craftsman, for he had but half a heart in either cause. (2-3)

As Sieglinde Lemke points out, dualism present within Modernism was due to "the racist imagination [which] conflated these two versions of alterity [African American and white] and defined people of African descent as irrational, uncivilized, and not-yet-modern" (4-5). Black mainstream Modernist ideology insisted on debunking racial conceptualizations of African Americans, which certainly reproduced notions of white Modernism as a proof of imagined authenticity. Far be it to claim that Black Modernism is simply the reproduction of white Modernism, but, as James De Jongh insists, parallels can certainly be detected such as the "chaotic cultural, political, even metaphysical ambiguities" (qtd. in *Crossroads* xv).

Hurston, on the other hand, represents a split within Black Modernism as she distances herself from both white and Black mainstream Modernism. Distancing is not negation per se, but the creative, that is, reinterpreting, use of Modernist notions of both. Hybridity renders Hurston's works Modernist (see Lemke 15) and establishes a nonplace in Augé's and Munn's sense. Technically, Hurston's expertise in anthropology provides her with a unique view that shapes her modernism and undergirds her cultural politics:

> While borrowings from ethnography and from the aesthetics of non-Western cultures are hallmarks of high modernist style, these appropriations typically serve to dramatize or add weight to the deracinated artist's view of modernity at the center. Hurston's appropriations, on the other hand, bolster her call for recognition of the

ties that bind the center's experience of modernity to disavowed experiences of modernity on the periphery that would otherwise be passed off as pre-modern survivals. (Sorensen)

In this way, her nonplace-like places such as the muck in *Their Eyes* or the site of the barbecue in *Jonah's*—both lower-class, rural, but, more importantly, African (American), thus supposedly *uncivilized* and *primitive*—serve a centripetal function in that they display inclusion of marginal places in the cultural framework.

The criticism that her works incited (see West 108-21) sheds light on the nature of Hurston's cultural politics. As a matter of fact, Richard Wright's criticism of *Their Eyes Were Watching God* can be taken as reference to Hurston's world as a cultural other in this respect: "Miss Hurston *voluntarily* continues in her novel the tradition that was *forced* upon the Negro in the theatre, that is, the minstrel technique that makes the 'white folks' laugh. Her characters [. . .] swing like a pendulum eternally in that safe and narrow orbit in which America likes to see the Negro live: between laughter and tears" (251). Hurston, the anthropologist, knew that the segment of the black population she apparently idealized was declining and in minority (Carby 121), but her mode of representation emanated from the dominant mode of anthropological representation of the time. As Hazel V. Carby reminds us, Hurston used her expertise in anthropology to "provid[e] a professional point of view" (124).

Concomitantly, *imitation* and *masking*, two terms that Lynda Marion Hill uses to describe Hurston's cultural politics, raise the question of authenticity, but in my line of analysis, they lend Hurston's cultural universe a nonplace-like character for its trickster quality. Indeed the cultural performances in places like the muck, roads, or the tie-camp in the two novels render imitation a trickster strategy. The very criticism that Hurston continues the tradition of minstrel shows with their supposed stock characters and stereotypical atmospheres falls in with "the Negro's universal mimicry" ("Characteristics" 49), which Hurston identifies in her ethnographic research. I much rather agree with Hill that Hurston employs the strategy of masking as "a vehicle through which African-Americans transmute the minstrel mask into cultural performances which are at once, linguistic, artistic, and politically informed" (xxiii). Masking her cultural space as a static world that seems to reinforce racial stereotypes carries on the tradition of disguised resistance to racialist conceptualizations of the African American self, or, as Hurston, calls it a "feather-bed resistance" (*Mules* 4). Her imitation of the lower class and rural people establishes for Hill the originality of Hurston's works; furthermore, it provides Hurston with a toolbox of social criticism. In this way, she is able to neatly criticize "social scientific explanations of cultural diffusion and assimilation" by, for instance, reconceptualizing stereotypes (Hill 37).

Mimicry was an existing form of cultural expression also supported by white patrons, who demanded the supply of African American cultural production reinforcing cultural stereotypes. Hurston and other African American writers, as Brian Carr and Tova Cooper suggest, "because of the commodification of African-American bodies and cultural forms persisting as slavery's legacy, were acutely aware of the inevitable cooptation of their selfrepresentations within a system of capitalist exchange and racialized patronage" (288). The survival of African Americans as writers in the literature market depended on their ability to adapt to white expectations. Hurston's *mimicry* can then be explained as programmatic inauthenticity that veils over authentic cultural performances.

Despite the apparent inauthentic façade Hurston employs as a cultural performance itself, the other aspect of her nonplace-like cultural space is, what Carby depreciatively calls, Hurston's "discursive displacement of contemporary social crises [by] the creation of a discourse of the 'folk' as a *rural* people" (Carby 12). Quite the contrary to what Carby means by her statement, for Hurston, beyond the fact that African Americans are rooted in southern black culture, the replacement of African Americans in this cultural realm serves as the solution of the urban crisis. What seems Hurston's antiurban sentiment is a response to the Modernist crisis that for African Americans is clearly tainted with selfconceptualization, the struggle against racism, and social problems of urbanization. Placing the problematization of African Americans in a southern rural environment, that is, Florida—truly enough, idealized and pastoral as it appears—Hurston establishes a space that geographically relocates them in a space that effects politically an antidiscourse regarding the expectations of the politics of the urban Black intelligentsia.

Nevertheless Hurston's cultural politics places her clearly in the centre of the Harlem Renaissance and in the Modernist discourse: her concept of culture shows that Hurston's view integrates both the modern, relativist approach to culture and the Lockean concept of the *New Negro* with a "new psychology" and "new spirit" (Locke 3). Hurston's Janie and John crystallize subjects with an integrated cultural background with autonomous cultural identities in mostly chemically pure black environments. Janie's new subjectivity is stunningly explicated at the end of her journey: "The light in her hand was like a spark of sun-stuff washing her face in fire" (*Their Eyes* 183). The religious connotation of the scene[22] elevates Janie with all her insight to a position which grants her authentic identity.

---

[22] Moses's face was shining after an encounter with God, when he received the Ten Commandments: "And till Moses had done speaking with them, he put a vail on his face. But when Moses went in before the LORD to speak with him, he took the vail off, until he came out. And he came out, and spake unto the children of Israel that which he was commanded. And the children of Israel saw the face of Moses, that the skin of Moses' face

In fact, her concept of culture becomes the source of her modernism: as Leif Sorensen claims, a "mode of modernism that, instead of dramatizing the perils or pleasures of a particular totalized modernity, creates a discursive space in which multiple claims to modernity compete with one another" (par. 4). According to Sorensen, her diversity concept relies on a twofold basis, that of racial and gender marginalization manifested already in her ethnographic writing; and so her experience of marginalization along these lines during her research trips must have made her understand struggle within culture.

The primary evidence against the claim that Hurston would return to the minstrel tradition is that her cultural space maintains the heterogeneous character she gives account of in *Mules and Men* and *Tell My Horse*. As Hill points out, "she left every inch of contradiction and ambiguity in place. The result is that her work constantly reminds us of unresolved tensions surrounding any mention of racial, cultural, social, and sexual differences and of the power struggles" (xxxi). Concomitantly, her writing mirrors her research findings as she allows her ethnographic gaze to penetrate the places of her characters; as well as it reflects her selfevaluation *vis-à-vis* white and black social spaces, and her positioning in the midst of her research. As her nonplaces suggest, including the masculine games in the tie-camp and the work songs in the construction site for railroads in *Jonah's*, she works with the cultural information borrowed and distilled from her ethnographic knowledge. Hurston's cultural space appears, in fact, as ambivalent as that of her time.

4.2. Nonplace in the Two Novels

The heterogeneity of her cultural space is revealed by the spatial orientations despite Hurston's masking and undermines her presumed inauthenticity. John's close identification with nature proposes this view: "Ah'll tip on 'cross de good Lawd's green. Ah'll give mah case tuh Miss Bush and let Mother Green stand mah bond" (95). John's confession not only suggests a well-anchored cultural identity, but also an orientation yet distanced even from mainstream Southern black cultural space.

Nonplaces thus have a clear function in Hurston's work and come to the foreground powerfully in *Jonah's*. As John keeps running away, he always flees from something somewhere to elsewhere, which is constituted as a safe haven in the unknown from the point of view of status quo society. Alf Pearson, the

---

shone [. . .]" (KJV, Ex. 34: 32-35). Janie's shining face detaches her from the black community also in a moral way: just like Moses, she becomes the carrier of knowledge, a prophet to announce a new phase in the community's life. At the same time, Janie's shining face is Hurston's ultimate criticism of her community: Moses's veil was not understood by the Jews (see 2 Cor. 3:14-16) and the shining face denoting liberty (2 Cor. 3:16) is not accepted by the Harlem community either.

formal slaveowner, verbalizes the normative expectations of transparent space: "Stop running away. Face things out" (67), which aims at keeping John in his place, that is, in the visible (even if he confesses later that "John, distance is the only cure for certain diseases" [99]). At the same time, the strangeness of nonplaces proves to be affirming for refugees from the transparent. As it is narrated, "Distance was escape" (47). The positive approach to nonplaces is supported by the title of the book itself. Jonah in the Bible left the city of Nineveh and found shelter under a gourd vine provided by God "to give shade for his head to ease his discomfort" (NIV, Jonah 4:6). Nonplaces elsewhere, that is, not in the normative framework of social space, but in opposition to it, are regarded in *Jonah's* as something positive and individual(izing).

In this framework, Hurston inverts the meaning of roads by transforming them from gendered space denoting masculine mobility (as opposed to female situatedness in domestic space) into a cultural performance of detour, that is, a nonplace, where the paradigm of social space is not binding. When it is stated in *Their Eyes* that, on leaving Killicks's place, "[Janie] turned wrongside out just standing there and feeling [and] hurried out of the front gate and turning south" (30-31), it is shown how her body is identified with what the road denotes. Through turning inside out, attempting to find realization of her inner life in space for the first time; she temporarily resolves the "imbalance between internal and external space" (351) Stuart Aitken and Christopher Lukinbeal talk about regarding road films. Janie breaks away from masculine social space, and enters the "antithesis to a familiar place" (Steinke 3), which is not incorporated into the order of society. She feels liberated for two important reasons: a) here she can reminisce about the vision encountered under the pear tree at Nanny's place and accentuating her subjectivity; b) from the point of view of Hurston's cultural politics, Janie's turning south renders her quest for identity visible in cultural terms. As she starts her journey heading south, she not only begins to reconnect symbolically to a region, but also commences to quest for her self.

A similar conceptualization of the road is also present in *Jonah's*. John leaves Ned's place "singing a new song and stomping the beats" (12). The Big Creek visualizes an "intermediate point" (141) and "a hub of irresponsibility" (Archer 142) which stands in a sharp contrast to the barrenness of the previous place. It is not only filled with life and vitality, but it appears familiar with its naturalness and even coziness: the vivid description and the emotionally suggestive words are accompanied by the emergence of African memories embodied by "the drums of the Creek" (12). The freedom John experiences is grounded in both the relief from "place-based sedentarism" (Aitken and Lukinbeal 351)[23] accentuated by Ned's oppressive nature and "disengaged

---

[23] In their essay Stuart C. Aitken and Christopher Lee Lukinbeal examine "home-based masculinity" and "resistance to mere adequacy through travel and the road" (351) in road movies. They identify tension between "place-based masculinity" and "disassociated

mobility" (351) flavored by the hope for selffulfillment. Realized outside the boundaries of social space, the in-betweenness of the Creek cannot be conceptualized by either the world that we get to know through Ned's place or Pearson's place. Exactly this character of the roads and locales in nature renders them transient (and rigid for social space's incapability to conceptualize them), that is, subjective and open for temporary inhabiting. John enlivens and inscribes the place as he passes through it: for example, he incorporates the place into his world when his selfexulting masculinity is shown in the fact that "he breathe[s] lustily" (12) and swims across the river naked.

The muck in *Their Eyes* symbolizes Hurston's antipicture of society and her primary means of "solidify[ing] a notion of racial authenticity in southern rural geographies" (Favor 16). The transience Augé ascribes to nonplaces becomes here visible: the muck is filled with people of many different origins from time to time, as the jobs of the season allow. As it is narrated, "They came in wagons from way up in Georgia and they came in truck loads from east, west, north and south. Permanent transients with no attachments and tired looking men with their families and dogs in flivvers" (125). The land is not claimed by any, homogeneous social space as in the case of Eatonville, or the white cities; much rather, through the mobility of the people it becomes dynamically changing itself, depending on those who inhabit it for the time being. In the democratic atmosphere of social juxtaposition, Hurston accounts for a web of places and temporary social ties that in a nonhierarchical way interconnect the workers. The political content becomes even more relevant if the proletarian fiction of Richard Right and Langston Hughes is seen as the other pole of the spectrum. While Hurston also addresses implicitly the urban crisis African Americans have to face, she emphasizes a radically different African American self embedded in African American culture precipitated by the cultural space of the Everglades. As Mary Helen Washington claims, Hurston writes about "the survival of love, loyalty, joy, humor, and affirmation, as well as tragedy in black life [because] she believed in the beauty of black expression and traditions and in the psychological wholeness of black life" (138).

In fact, African American cultural space is what connects the people of African descent in the Everglades. The cultural artifacts that reflect Hurston's anthropological research, as well as around which the social space of the muck evolves; suggest a deeper structure of connectedness. Jooks, games, the blues, and storytelling establish a context freed from "restrictive organizational structure" (McGowan 1) in which every member of the Everglades society can let his/her voice be heard. As it is put in regarding Janie, "Only here, she could

---

masculinity" both part of the patriarchal myth. However, the latter also carries the possibility of male hysteria. For Hurston's John the road brings on a liberating experience as it "supplants place-identity with a personal geography that is based upon movement and mobility" (351) as do roads for men in films examined in the essay.

listen and laugh an even talk some herself if she wanted to" (*Their Eyes* 128). Hurston identifies a deeper African American stratum that also appears in other works of hers: the throbbing and pulsing of Africanisms crystallized on the muck, for instance, in "the subtle but compelling rhythms of the Bahaman drummers" (133) or fire dances (146).

Despite the seeming overdetermination of her political philosophy, Hurston maintains the tension in her imagined society. Class struggle triggered by color politics appears with Mrs. Turner's "internalized racism" (Haddox par. 27), who represents that "Us ought to class off" (135), whereby she also admits a sublime and other-oriented racial discourse. Gender struggle enters with Nunkie; however, here it is more balanced, as it is Janie, who once claims Tea Cake and beats him, and another time Tea Cake behaves possessively in front of other men.

Despite the tension manifesting the race-gender-class trichotomy, the Everglades society remains pluralistic and democratic. Janie once becomes conscious of "a band of Seminoles passing by" who she "[h]as seen [. . .] several times" (146). It happens before the hurricane strikes, during which the Everglades with all possible differences is literally washed together. The frequent presence of Native Americans, as well as the way their procession is described, that is, they pass by naturally without fear as parts of the scene, suggest that they form a part of the cultural landscape in Hurston's conception despite their apparent otherness and subverted position. Furthermore, the Bahaman workers embody not only another segment of the Everglades social space further coloring the demographic spectrum, but also they are integrated in it as they are "gradually drawn into the American [that is, mainland] crowd" (146). Clearly and especially when the analogous scenes in *Jonah's* are considered, when the "Saws" "quit hiding out to hold their dances" (146), their integration into the African American cultural plethora becomes palpable. The folk religious notions maintained from African religions further crystallize an Africanist connection. On the advent of the hurricane Lias says, for instance, "If Ah never see you no mo' on earth, Ah'll meet you in Africa" (148). It was the belief of slaves that when they die, they return to Africa. The recollection of African beliefs and tradition, and foremost their praxis by mainland African Americans engender a deep structure of a shared cultural space.

In *Jonah's* the muck's democratic vision detectable in *Their Eyes Were Watching God* does not materialize as an overt political agenda. However, it is present in an even more culturally implosive way, "clearing away competing historical explanations from different times, places, and identities" (Hughes-Warrington 75).[24] On Pearson's place there takes place a black festival after

---

[24] Marnie Hughes-Warrington addresses the issue of revision in history, which she identifies as a nonplace for its non-sequential nature. She acknowledges the heterotopic character of history and the juxtaposition of rival histories. As she claims, "Spatial imagery and

cotton picking. Hurston uses this event as almost an ethnographic account of an anthropologist, yet in this line of analysis the place described gains relevance as alternative to social space. For one, people come here from their homes, that is, from their point of view they go to a place undermining their time-space disposition. It is narrated that people stream from three different plantations (28). The designation of their home as "plantation" is also relevant, since the novel stages events after the abolition of slavery, but the word yet connotes the subservient position of blacks. It is also heightened by the remark that "Alf Pearson gave the hands two hogs to barbecue" (28). While the whole event is presented as an integrated and ahistorical happening, the festive event also happens as hide-aways used to in the time of slavery when blacks stole away to secret places of sacred grounds.

For the Africanisms present, the event possesses a transpatial character, which is why the negative-space-like nature in Munn's sense is furthermore complemented by a heterotopous character. The positioning of the event is relevant: the barbecuing takes place on Pearson's plantation, which has a transparent character, similar to the "panopticon" described by Foucault in his *Discipline and Punish*. As it is, the plantation provides the framework and conditions thus what can take place there, as well as in what manner. Pearson's person becomes, in this way, the node of possible actions overseen by him as the plantation can be regarded as the embodiment of his self, and, in a likewise manner, his body as the signifier of the semantics of the social space of the plantation. Pearson is presented as the frame, remaining an outsider, yet omniscient simultaneously, and staged as the benevolent benefactor, signifying hierarchy but also distance.

The juxtaposition of the two, seemingly mutually exclusive spaces, that is, African American cultural space and Pearson's transparent social space, which is constructed on racial bias and embodies white aristocratic values; suggests relative independence and integrity of both spaces. This derives from the presentation of African American cultural space as an authentic space intruding into the Euro-American spatial framework, yet with considerable "freedom from the constraints of proximity" (Arefi 180). The insistence on African religious elements heighten the sense of distinctiveness and on standing apart from the white cultural framework. The difference establishes palpable boundaries between the two spaces. The scene appears a condensation of the society of the muck in *Their Eyes*, which there, however, becomes a geographical constant for its geographical separation from both black and white social spaces. The series of events underline that, apart from the religio-cultural character lending an unmistakably African atmosphere to this event, the types of social interaction

---

language are used to construct temporary discursive spaces in which rival historiographies are excluded [. . .]" (75). Temporality and detachment from other homogenizing contexts render her these discursive spaces akin with nonplaces.

firmly anchor it in African American culture—a clear indication of Hurston's negation of minstrelsy and her "defiance of popular representations of the black folk" (Trombold 91).

Inwardly African American cultural space is implosive, on the one hand, through an act of transposition of Africa into Alabama and "tactical redefinition of the meaning" (86), rendering the scene of the event heterotopous. There is not any oscillation between the two worlds: due to missing anchorage in social space, just as nonplaces for Mahyar Arefi, the barbecue "lacks any chronological connection to a broader physical, cultural or emotional context" (183). On the other hand, the framework is established as homogeneous within, through African American cultural praxis and artifacts. Dancing, in the first place, but also the musical instruments (e.g., hands, feet, and drums) serve as the performative tools to create the cultural framework, that is, "hollow-hand clapping" and "heel and toe stomping" (30) as reminders of both tribal vitality and slavery-time congeniality.

Even though sacred places of Hurston's religio-cultural space form my main focus of the next chapter, it must be mentioned that sacred places have also a nonplace-like character not for transience, but for their essential otherness that denotes them as timeless and detached from social space. In Hurston's fiction religion has a definite role in the construction of social space; however, by incorporating also non-Christian elements in it, the binary of place versus nonplace regarding religion receives a definite function. Often Hurston connects this issue to questions of morality, but the treatment of non-Christian places remains ambiguous. In *Their Eyes* specifically Starks's acceptance of the help of the root doctor indicates an irresolvable estrangement from his own living environment, since he seeks solution elsewhere, not within the given and accepted cultural framework. As about the identity of the root doctor, it is stated that "[Starks] had been scornful of root-doctors and all their kind, but now she [that is, Janie] saw a faker from over around Altamonte Springs, hanging around the place almost daily" (78). The treatment accepted from the Voodoo man places him outside social space. Janie endowed with the power of moral judgment, which is shown by the inversion of her position in the house by this time, looks down on the doctor as a faker and scoundrel, whose legitimacy as well as role in the spatial framework is questioned. The negative evaluation of the root doctor is also described by his physical distancing from the clear boundaries of the imagined cultural space of Eatonville, and his positioning in the indefinite.[25]

---

[25] Hill argues that Starsk's reliance on the root doctor and Janie's on modern medicine refers to an unrecoverable gap between the two, just as Janie's anticonventional behavior and traditionalism are irreconcilable (xxv). Even though Janie's use of modern medicine can be connected to progress as her performance can signify a movement away from traditional race-gender-class conceptions, it cannot be justified that this instance proves Janie's choice

Hideouts, on the other hand, are brought into the cultural space of African Americans and become integrated into the central values and cultural performances of the cultural space of the muck. When the invitation is formulated that "You better stay heah, man. Big jumpin' dance tuhnight right heah, when it fair off" (148), it can be inferred that the ancient dance marks a festive event for all "hands" of the muck. Hurston connects action to an African American primordial self that is but a denotation of African American subjectivity for her. Subjectivity is able to activate African Americanness in a trickster-like manner, which is able to transform space into its own likeness. As it is narrated in *Jonah's* after the barbecue at Pearson's: "The fire died. The moon died. The shores of Africa receded" (31). The end of the barbecue indicates the inwardly implosive nature of this cultural space as evolving and relapsing with the fire, as well as its elsewhereness or displacement as its framework is curtailed by time and space in a lack of "historical connectedness" (Arefi 183).

The authenticity of the scene can be questioned due to its apparently idealized character, which appears to extinguish social and interpersonal tension. The barbecue is undoubtedly sutured into the narrative, where it, as an "extra-historical creation" (Trombold 86), almost unexpectedly explodes obliterating anything unlike its character; however, the importance of the scene lies in establishing a space that melts down the properties of white and black social space. The awareness of the white frame embodied by Pearson ceases and the differences based on gender and class in the African American community are not retained. In fact, it is not possible to recover where the whole event takes place on the basis of the subsequent actions for the contours of the plantation dissolve completely.

Similarly to the muck or hideouts, the tie-camp in *Jonah's* further implores Hurston's concept of an inwardly implosive nonplace. It is deliberately positioned elsewhere even within black cultural space and has important religio-cultural ramifications. Presenting an antipicture of urbanism and black middle-class America; and thus, generally, of a homogeneous, static, and transparent society, Hurston constitutes the tie-camp, a nonplace that "*exceed*[s] the logic of place" (Osborne 189), as a site of wilderness experience, staging it as heterogeneous and pluralistic.

The cross-section delineated by time and space is an exact realization of the barbecue on a daily and weekly (that is, Saturday nights) basis. As the barbecue is organized around the fire at night, the organic gatherings in the tie-camp are also conducted after work at night, however, growingly around John's personality. By excelling in all types of African American cultural interaction in

---

of the modern in opposition to African American traditions. A proof against it is the fact that Janie is informed about hoodoo practice to the extent that she makes use of it in establishing her personal spatiality, especially as the tree can be taken as a voodoo symbol.

the camp, John manages to do the very same as during the crossing of the Creek: he transforms space into his likeness as "he was the center of camp life" (61)— proving openness of this nonplace in the sense that it is in fact transitory and welcoming regarding inscription. He does individually what in the barbecue is constructed on group level: he inscribes his own spatiality, whereby the tie-camp becomes a denotation of his extended self. Praxis, that is, not only work, which establishes the space of the camp initially through the rhythmic swing of axes and the accompanying chant of the workers (60), but also cultural forms such as wrestling, chinning the bar, balancing axes, or storytelling; enables him to draw in the space around. He does what the fire establishes during the barbecue previously. In this sense, his body delimits space as a symbol and as a means of action. Even though John ultimately inscribes space through action, that is, fighting, when he remains unchallenged, and his space uncontested for the time being; the symbolism used by Hurston is more revealing. It is recounted that "he could stand like a cross, immobile for several seconds with an axe muscled out in each hand" (61). The moment establishes John as the primary agent of the space of the tie-camp. The symbolism of the scene reifies beyond his capability of holding the axes, proving his physical strength; the scene's religious connotations with his statue similar to the crucified Christ. The two axes establish him as the battle axe of God, both emphasizing his univocal position of the community, as well as foreshadowing his future as a servant of God.[26] Later he confesses his calling into the ministry, claiming that "God done called me tuh preach" after the psalm "He's a Battle-Axe in de Time Uh Trouble" (111).

Even if Hurston's space may appear rigid and inauthentic from the outside, inwardly it is based on transience. In *Jonah's* this becomes visible in both the main character's journey, as a black way of cultural detour, and the safe haven of the tie-camp-like places. The latter precipitate a before-unaccounted-for cultural pluralism, which allows spatial paradigms and stories to co-exist and not only to collide. The nonplace aspect enters as a shared attribute of non-belongingness as a result of loss of a "sense of consequence" (Kunstler 246), which, at the same time, establishes a collective third space on a meta-level. The tie-camp or the muck cannot be claimed by one single spatial paradigm. They form thus nonplaces from the point-of-view of the mainstream spatiality for their unintelligibility, on the other hand, they are hybrid space through their antisocial character in Augé's sense. The antisocial character is to be understood as the lack of homogeneity that would enable the ordering of this space into a well-defined spatial paradigm. The striking aspect of Hurston's conceptualization of these places is the heterotopical network of free social interaction.

---

[26] Jeremiah 51:20: "Thou art my battle axe and weapons of war: for with thee will I break in pieces the nations, and with thee will I destroy kingdoms" (KJV).

Nonplaces for Hurston thus represent hybrid places open for inscription. This rather Modernist notion is the means to overcome the constraints of white and black social and mainstream cultural spaces, on both individual and group levels. Indeed, apparent mimicry is deconstructed through the tension generated by nonplaces. With the help of nonplaces (and the books are but such places), Hurston manages to establish a "discursive space" (Sorensen par. 4) within Black (and white) Modernism and apart from it. Thus by offering an alternative space in the South, she contests the framework of Black Modernism. Hurston does so consciously and offers a nonplace that appears to conform to white expectations—but in a trickster-like fashion; however, especially through the schisms built in her space, she also distances her space from the ideals of black urbanity. More specifically, Hurston's strategy in establishing her cultural space as a nonplace and employing nonplaces within it as primary constructive building blocks hybridizes the concept of cultural space *par excellence.* Nonplaces represent dynamizing and multiple inversions of cultural precipitations and conceptions, be it place, like the South, African American community, or the African American self. At the same time, and this marks perhaps foremost Hurston's authenticity, her masking of space, place, and self as timeless and seemingly reinforcing cultural stereotypes proves subversive of racialized conceptions and displaces assimilationist creeds.

5. Black Sacred Cosmos: Liminal Places and Hurston's Religio-Cultural Framework

Liminality plays an important role in Zora Neale Hurston's religio-cultural space as it parallels an understanding of African American life in terms of rituals. Marginal places postulate a peripherized, individual consciousness—but always-already contextualized in a broader socio-cultural space. From a religio-cultural point of view, *Jonah's Gourd Vine* shows the connection between liminal places and the submergence/emergence motif in African American visions from a religio-cultural point of view; while *Their Eyes Were Watching God* elaborates explicitly on the meaning of initiation narratives displaying African American cosmology, imbuing the whole of African American culture. Liminal places and visions play a seminal role in traditional African American community in that at the first glance they represent marginal discourses; yet prove essential in the selfverification of the community itself. Antithetical to the main discourse of the community, they construct a set of essential structural elements.

Hurston's theology appears difficult to discuss because of her apparent syncretic colorfulness and seeming refusal of Christianity. Daughter of an Eatonville preacher, on the one hand; and, as she refers to herself, "Conjure Queen" ("To Langston Hughes" 124), on the other, she moves between religious paradigms to incorporate all into her religio-cultural space. Her religiosity does not show theologically informed conceptions, but much rather a cosmological framework deriving from an understanding of a distinct African American folk culture. Her view of religions apparently abhors any reverence of the divine:

> The unreachable and therefore the unknowable always seems divine—hence, religion. People need religion because the great masses fear life and its consequences. Its responsibilities weigh heavy. Feeling a weakness in the face of great forces, men seek alliance with omnipotence to bolster up their feeling of weakness, even though the omnipotence they rely upon is a creature of their own minds. (*Dust Tracks* 277-78)

Her explanation of religious sentiments detaches her from established religious forms and, at the most, allows for individual, active (not passive) alterations. But even though, in an antiauthoritarian way, she turns away from submissive religiosity, she nevertheless yields to infinity: "As for me, I do not pretend to read God's mind. If He has a plan of the universe worked out to the smallest detail, it would be folly for me to presume to get down on my knees and attempt to revise it. [. . .] Prayer seems to me a sign of weakness, and an attempt to avoid, by trickery, the rules of the game as laid down" (278). In her flowing rhetoric, Hurston refuses supplication, yet testifies about a cosmological view that places her in a divine world order. In this view, every person has a clearly defined, immutable place in the universe. Hurston's theology does not necessarily impart a deterministic creed (or one of predestination), but, instead, it affirms a cosmological order; and the human quest blends into it: "When the consciousness we know as life ceases, I know that I shall still be part and parcel of the world" (*Dust Tracks* 279).

Hurston's notion of religiosity justifies dealing with her sacred space as a distinct religio-cultural paradigm. In fact, her cultural space bears characteristics similar to Eric C. Lincoln and Lawrence H. Mamiya's concept of "black sacred cosmos," which does not simply denote an African American religious worldview (2), but also treats it as a totality bearing distinctively African American characteristics. Similarly to Lincoln and Mamiya's identification of the relevance of the particular black experience in America, whereby they emphasize the particularity, authenticity, and cultural politics of black religiosity; Hurston employs the African American cultural context to construct an authentic religio-cultural space in both *Jonah's* and *Their Eyes*.

Authentication of her cosmos equals the anthropologist's depiction of everyday life interwoven with religiosity and religion itself as "multidimensional space to be broken down regarding public or interior aspects" (Brown 102)—ultimately established in relation to two poles: the official and liminal. The former refers to "absolute sacred space," that is, "*permanent* sacral places" (Keményfi 39). The latter constitutes "relative space," unfixed, and describes a process, sanctification, and an experience of space (38). Thus liminal places signify ambiguous entities, since they often denote non-Christian (hoodoo/voodoo) places as well as places of conversion. Thirdly, praying grounds appear as liminal places, as places of encounter with, what Rudolph Otto calls, the "numinous" (7). They appear incorporated into official sacred space, yet maintain a high degree of individuality: they are inscribed outside the church walls but within the official Christian paradigm. Thus, beyond official or institutionalized religion, Hurston's black sacred cosmos also incorporates folk religious phenomena. The two realms together shape an integrated whole. Folk religious aspects denote liminal places as structural units within the black sacred cosmos.

Arnold Van Gennep's theory of the triple sequence of separation, margin, and aggregation in initiation rites has much in common with Victor Turner's theory of liminality. In fact, Turner's liminal phase corresponds to Van Gennep's margin, both of which can be translated into the African American wilderness experience (or "vision quest" [see Heintzman]). In this threefold system the liminal signifies a transitory phase prior to the subject becoming a full member of the community:

The attribute of liminality or of liminal *personae* ("threshold people") are necessarily ambiguous, since this condition and these persons elude or slip through the network of classifications that normally locate states and positions in cultural space. Liminal entities are neither here nor there; they are betwixt and between the positions assigned and arrayed by law, custom, convention, and ceremonial. (Turner 95)

Since the attributes of the given socio-cultural space do not hold in liminal places, liminal subjects become temporarily outsiders to the group. Despite the inaccessibility of such places, they work as nonplaces on the margins of society, yet within it. As structural units these places have a connecting function in the in-between in spite of their non-alignment to social space: "During the intervening 'liminal' period, the characteristics of the ritual subject (the 'passenger') are ambiguous; he passes through a cultural realm that has few or none of the attributes of the past or coming state" (Turner 94).

Hurston describes then African American wilderness experience in detail in *Sanctified Church,* in which she explicitly elaborats on "coming through religion" (87). Channeled by the respective community, the ritual lasts usually for three days, by the end of which the candidate has gone through several dramatic revelations. Going through such a conversion experience serves for the novice as the threshold to emerge as a member of the community. Candidates retreat to secluded places to obtain the vision: "People, solemn of face, crept off to the woods to 'praying ground' to seek religion. Every church member worked on them hard, and there was great clamor and rejoicing when any of them 'come through' religion" (*Dust* 270). Such places are outside social space, only ritually connected to it—the power mechanisms of social space do not bind there. Wilderness experience represents an individual quest for an identity in the community and a threshold or nonplace of established *communitas.*

To prove worthiness of "induction into the regular community" (*Dust* 272) the candidates must undergo a test before the community. This test comprises an oral testimony, during which they present their vision; that is, tell a story of their conversion:

These visions are traditional. I knew them by heart as did the rest of the congregation, but still it was exciting to see how the converts would handle them. Some of them made up new details. Some of them would forget a part and improvise clumsily or fill up the gap with shouting. The audience knew, but everybody acted as if every word of it was new. (272)

Not the ripeness of faith, but the readiness and ability of the candidates to integrate into the black sacred cosmos are tested, which is a cultural act. These visions are appropriated to/within the social space as they are used as conventional patterns of expression and constitute a segment of the story-telling tradition.

Whereas Janie's journey in *Their Eyes* evolves through different alienating places, in *Jonah's* the process of submersion and emersion is less clearly present. John's journey, similarly to Janie's, is structured around places of margin, or liminal places, but emersion from these places bears manifold signification, as if condensing Eliade's threefold differentiation of initiation rites.[27] John's experience of liminal places is strongly connected to sexuality. This is manifested as early as children's games. On Alf Pearson's place black children play hide-and-seek games, during which John hides at secluded places. Two times he hides with two different girls and the third time, when the third girl approaches him, the game stops abruptly. This foreshadows his promiscuous lifestyle, which is always accompanied by hide-aways with different women, as well as it delineates the would-be structure of his life. He has three wives later on, the last of which loses him abruptly.

The number three has a mythic quality for Hurston. In her discussion of visions, she emphasizes the relevance of the number three: "Three days is the traditional period for seeking the vision" (*Sanctified* 85), and again "Three is the holy number and the call to preach always comes three times" (86). The number three reappears in *Their Eyes* also: Janie has three husbands, thus the three stations of Janie's journey lines up with the African American way of coming through religion; in *Jonah's* the number of waiting time is also three (27), John encounters the train three times (the last time the train kills him).

Furthermore, the role of liminal places is emphasized by the fact that such places frame the narrative. After the hide-and-seek game John finds "a tiny clearing hidden by trees" (25), which becomes a praying ground, where he prays for the first time. In fact, the way John approaches the sacred echoes Róbert Keményfi's concept of the sacred: John's mental functioning changes when he recognizes the sacred place as such for its qualitative differences from the profane (36). His words characterize his whole life torn between guilt and reconciliation: "if you find any lurkin' sin in and about mah heart please pluck it out and cast it intuh de sea uh fuhgitfulness whar it'll never rise tuh condemn me in de judgment" (25). His words are almost exactly the same as his last prayer accounted for in her third wife's, Sally's bedroom at the end of the book, where he asks for forgiveness.

Liminal places are integrated into a moral geography (*see* Dixon 1); however, this feature turns out dubious. Hurston refuses to justify John's debauchery, and connects hoodoo to immorality, situating it on the margins of

---

[27] The three types of initiation comprise puberty rites, tribal initiation, and initiation into an age group (*Rites and Symbols* 2).

the African American community. Hattie, John's second wife, for example, conjures him with the help of root doctors. Clearly, Hattie's evil character leads her to employ practices outside the norms of African American social space. The positioning of the root doctors reveals, however, also their status: both hoodoo men are decentralized from the point of view of social space; that is, positioned elsewhere, not in Eatonville.

The description of hoodoo places also stands in stark contrast to the places of official religion. While the Baptist church in Plant City is described as "the big white building that Baptist pride had erected" (*Jonah's* 186), An' Dangie Dewoe lives in a hut that "squatted low and peered at the road from behind a mass of Palma Christi and elderberry" (125). The difference between the place of official religion and, from the perspective of Christianity, a nonplace becomes palpable. Big white church buildings in a central position denote power and become an emblem of social space (see Wedam 49) and a token against the "privatization of place" (Sheldrake 126). In contrast to that, the conjure man's hut seems an inversion of the church in a rural setting. The nature of the hoodoo ritual renders it private and individual ("unrepresentable" in Bhabha's sense [37]), while the Church sermons depict a public and collective event based on mass interaction and a process of bearing up—the development of the African American sermon to its final ecstatic resolution. The structuring of the narrative posits this place to be immoral and marginal, in the first place, by revealing also that the fact that Hattie uses hoodoo to conjure both John and Lucy (the next chapter starts with the sentence: "Lucy was lying sick" [*Jonah's* 127]; and soon after that she dies).

The hoodoo hut is not presented as ultimately negative, however. Firstly, the hoodoo hut is connected to prehistoric times; secondly, deeply embedded in nature—both conceptualizations lying in the heart of African American culture, which is emphasized throughout the book. For example, when John has to flee from a lynching mob, he exclaims, "Ah'll tip on 'cross de good Lawd's green. Ah'll give mah case tuh Miss Bush and let Mother Green stand mah bond" (95). He emphasizes the traditionally protective and liberating conceptualization of nature. Furthermore, the constant reference to (prehistoric) Africanisms sheds light on Hurston's Africanist understanding of African American culture as a direct derivation of African culture in a constant mold.

Places of conversion are treated positively and clearly integrated into Christian sacred space as liminal places. Such a place is the revival meeting John conducts several times. Even though not much is narrated about such meetings, the incorporation of such places into black Christianity is signified by the evaluative contrast between the revival meeting and the hoodoo hut (140), as well as by the fact that the revival meeting is conducted by a preacher, the capstone of the community. These liminal places appear as "reconciled space" (Sheldrake 28) for they depict egalitarian regarding human relations, as they provide the framework needed to experience the numinous. Both European religious roots and the African American tradition of shouting can be detected in this phenomenon, but the fact that they bridge the gap between the transparency of absolute sacred space and the relativity and individualistic character of liminal places renders them important in Hurston's cosmology.

A third-space-like aspect of Christian sacred space can be detected in the revival meetings—rendering them parallel with praying grounds, which retain their individualistic nature. Praying grounds appear not just liminal in the sense that they embody marginal places, where the numinous can be experienced; but also hybrid constructions. This is the case despite the fact that candidates are conditioned culturally to choose certain places as "imago mundi" to use Eliade's coinage, that is, a tree or a clearing; but such places can be established anywhere. In Turner's footstep, such places can be regarded as "liminoid," since they can appear even within transparent social space, and can, for a moment, reinscribe space in De Certeau's sense. One time John is praying on his knees and "the empty house threw back his resonant tones like a guitar box" (52). The house's character changes when transposed into the sacred as totality, its emptiness referring to spiritual vacuity to be filled by the numinous, and the "guitar box" denoting not only the musicality of John's voice, but also the univocal nature of the place for the time being. John's experience echoes the phenomenology of contemplative practice, during which, as Sheldrake formulates it, "experiences of inward and outward, near at hand and far away, are synthesized so that distinctions between them cease to have any meaning" (128).

At the same time, Hurston hybridizes the morality of her sacred space. This can be detected by the conscious intermixing of different cultural paradigms. When John, for example, kills a cotton-mouth moccasin, he fights the male snake god, Damballah, thereby exhibiting masculine power in the "axis mundi." A similar sacred place evolves around trees. John and Lucy's love becomes sanctioned under a tree, and birth rituals are performed under trees when the naval cord gets buried there. Such transspatial elements render the apparent heteronomy of Hurston's sacred cosmos morally syncretic, but all the more culturally motivated.

The fusion can be detected in official sacred space also. Hurston calls John's funeral sermon a "barbaric requiem poem" (201). In the book the preaching as a genre comprises a cohesive device for the community, but this last sermon contains Africanist elements clearly transposed into it, which decentralizes the Christian discourse (with all its attributes of social space, be it race, gender, class, or even geography) by turning it into a syncretic "hierophany." "Self-revealing of the sacred" (Wasserstrom 36) precipitated in, cultural terms opens up a new and truly African American hybrid sacred space. In response to the preacher's call:

[. . .] the hearers wailed with a feeling of terrible loss. They beat upon the O-go-doe, the ancient drum. O-go-doe, O-go-doe, O-go-doe! Their hearts turned to fire and their shinbones leaped unknowing to the drum. Not Kata-Kumba, the drum of triumph, that speaks of great ancestors and glorious wars. Not the little drum of kidskin, for that is to dance with joy and to call to mind birth and creation, but O-go-doe, the voice of Death— that promises nothing, that speaks with tears only, and of the past. (202)

Hurston's technique may derive from her belief that "the Negro is not a Christian really" ("Characteristics" 56); but her embedding African Americans into Christianity renders this question more complex. Despite the fact that official sacred space refers to a different genealogy, which originally was superimposed, only later naturalized, adopted, and acculturated; Hurston seeks to juxtapose and syncretize both African religiosity and Christianity in her fiction, similarly to the praxis of African Americans, about whom she claims, "everything [the African American subject] touches is re-interpreted for his own use" (58). This understanding of black Christianity is clearly stated in *Jonah's*: once when John prays in church, "he roll[s] his African drum up to the altar, and call[s] his Congo Gods by Christian names" (89).

Sacred space for Hurston constitutes never merely the sacred ground of encounter with the divine, but it bears other significations as well. Sacred space is always cultural and social, or as Keményfi claims, "a category of societal life" (37), and hence revealing of the socio-cultural spaces at the same time. Thus, Hurston uses black Christianity and voodoo to represent her cultural politics also in sacred space. For example, Rachel Stein interprets the sacred tree of *Their Eyes* as a voodoo "image of spiritual and sexual ecstasy" (472), which becomes liminoid place to signify breaking norms of social space. Sheldrake's insistence on the particularity of places projects personal encounter with the sacred as it enables place to break away from the prescribed setting of social space. The marginality of non-Christian places aspires to totality, as opposed to partiality (Turner 106) of social space, quite strikingly, since experience is supposedly not channeled in non-Christian places; therefore subjectivity can be enlivened freely. The nature of place and its positioning coincide.

Furthermore, marginal places may also have a social character. Turner argues that in liminal places subjects form "communitas"[28] that can be described in terms of "spontaneity" and "immediacy" as well as homogeneity and

---

[28] Turner distinguishes between three types of communitas: existential or spontaneous communitas; normative communitas, which denotes already a "peduring social system"; and ideological communitas referring to utopias (132). The latter two types develop from existential communitas, which proves that "communitas itself develops a structure" (132).

unstructuredness (132), and in which there is "direct, immediate, and total confrontation of human identities" (132) without respect to social norms or hierarchy.

In *Jonah's*, apart from places like revival meetings, the social character of liminal sacred places is not emphasized. John undergoes conversion, which shows that, even though religious spaces and places are cohesively present in Hurston's sacred cosmos, his initiation represents ultimately a cultural category. Eliade also stresses the sacred nature of such an initiation: "*the puberty initiation represents above all the revelation of the sacred–and, for the primitive world, the sacred means not only everything that we now understand by religion, but also the whole body of the tribe's mythological and cultural traditions*" (3). The tie-camp for John constitutes the place of cultural immersion, from which he emerges with a mature cultural and masculine identity. The situatedness of the tie-camp in nature heightens its resemblance to the traditional wilderness experience; furthermore, the place is imbued with African American culture (games, sport, and telling stories). Third, the tie-camp is connected to the railroad and the locomotive, and a connection is thus established between place and John's masculine maturation: "Wall, you gwine learn [chew tobacco] 'cause you can't keep dis camp grub on yo' stomach lessen yuh do. Got tuh learn how tuh cuss too. Ah kin see you ain't nothin' but uh lad of uh boy. Mens on dese camps is full uh bulldocia 'til dey smell uh good size fist. Den dey dwindles down tuh nelly nothing" (60). The "structural outsiderhood" (Turner 134) denoted in this set of rules stands in sharp contrast to Alf Pearson's centralized place and the whiteness of the church, which also refers to the race discourse. The absence of characteristics of social space establishes a vacuum, which is hybridized into an egalitarian communitas. John has to negotiate identity by unlearning behavioral attitudes and thinking patterns to enter this communitas, where finally "his first real fight" (63) occurs as a clear assertion of his subjectivity.

The ritual nature of this immersion scene is also structured from a temporal point of view. The mythic number three of wholeness reappears here too. Even though the correlation between time and place is not clearly stated, John leaves for the tie-camp on the Alabama River after cotton picking in autumn (usually between August and October) and stays there until December. John spends three months away from the community at a secluded place, which parallels the temporal structure of the ritual acquisition of visions already mentioned.

For her confinement in domestic space and in the central places of African American community, Janie in *Their Eyes* does not appear to move back and forth on a large scale as John in *Jonah's*. Yet liminal places presented by the omnipresent tree and the muck in the Everglades occupy an important role in this novel, too.

The pear tree proves to be an overarching symbol in many ways in *Their Eyes*. From a religio-cultural point of view, the tree represents crossroads between the secular and sacred worlds in many senses. Glenda B. Weathers finds a replacement for the Biblical tree of knowledge in the trope of the pear tree: "In an innovative shift, Hurston replaces the legendary tree of knowledge, the apple tree, with an arguably more fitting symbol of the acquisition of carnal knowledge and sexual experience, the pear tree" (par. 5). The biblical tree of knowledge has a liminoid function within the sacred space of the Bible, since it represents a liminal place set apart within Paradise and Adam and Eve can obtain a new identity during the encounter with it. The pear tree differs from the biblical tree in that any encounter with the apple tree is considered a transgression, and it results not in reemergence in the sacred but in a ban out of it. The new subjectivity Adam and Eve gain through the deceptive activity of the snake presents a loss of contextualization in the sacred. In contrast, Hurston blurs a univocal understanding of the tree as a Christian symbol by substituting apples with pears and inverting the outcome of the encounter with the tree. The sensual symbol of the pear shows appropriation of and divergence from the Christian myth; and, even more strikingly, the tree leads Janie back to the sacred forgotten and remembered again (10) as she reemerges with a new consciousness within black sacred space and not outside it.

One cannot, therefore, argue for a single interpretation of the pear tree as a Christian symbol. Gerdès Fleurant describes trees as voodoo spiritual places dedicated to the voodoo deity Legba (12). In *Tell My Horse* Hurston herself accounts for the power of sacred trees: "People came to the palm tree and were miraculously cured and others were helped in various ways. The people began to worship the tree" (231). In general, trees are often employed in voodoo worship "as a vertical link between the sky, earth, and underworld" (Murphy 28). As axis mundi the tree becomes not only a possible access to the sacred, but also the interface, where devotees can maintain interstitial status.

The value of trees as liminal places is emphasized in Voodoo as Rachel Stein argues: "A syncretic religion, constantly evolving in response to changing cultural and social conditions, Voodoo encourages a view of human transformative possibilities, rather than externally fixed, eternally static identities. Crucially, Voodoo spirituality contests binaristic [sic] hierarchies with colonial structures that prove so damaging to black women" (469). Toni Morrison associates such transformative capacities with Africanism, insisting on the self-reflexive, meditative, as well as exploring nature of the "Africanist persona" (17). For Morrison "American Africanism makes it possible to say and not say, to inscribe and erase, to escape and engage, to act out and act on, to historicise and render timeless" (7). Stein, too, identifies similar features of Voodoo that are also connected to the tree in *Their Eyes*, as they present an opposition to subversive discourses such as the racial or gender dialectic. Also, the inherent characteristic of Voodoo to allow for transformation renders the pear tree the perpetuator of change. The tree becomes a place thus, where a "crossroad of consciousness" (De Weever 168) is experienced, presenting the possibility of change and choice.

Janie feels relieved and liberated when she ritually goes through the ecstatic experience after three days and "gaze[s] on a mystery" (*Their Eyes* 10). She hears "a flute song forgotten in another existence and remembered again" (10), remembering prehistoric/pre-Christian times. Just as "[John] has access to a pre-Christian cultural memory" (Hemenway 200) in *Jonah's*, Janie manages to enter an Africanist spirituality that proves to be life-transforming and presents her with a vision to be realized in the muck as imago mundi. This initiating experience (or foreshadowing initiation) enhanced by "border-crossing intermingling polarities" (Stein 469) so apt for Voodoo worship becomes a mapping of a spirituality or, much rather, a cosmological view to obtain.

Sexuality in the scene, then, can be understood as being a part of Voodoo transformation. Stein argues for such an understanding: Janie's final sexual immersion symbolizes a "sexual and spiritual union" (471), which symbolically refers to of "Damballah and his wife in sacred intercourse" (475). Sexuality serves a ritual function to lead to "a spiritual healing of the damaging divisions of body and soul, sex and spirit, male and female, animal and divine" (472). In this sense, temporary unification resolves Janie's "inner dislocation" (De Weever 168) and bestows upon her a hybrid identity of inbetweenness.

Besides the separation of the official/social and personal on a horizontal/geographical level in *Their Eyes,* separation is also established as a binary of inside and outside in a heterotopous manner. In Janie's case, the inside becomes both the demarcation of a marginal place from the point of view of social space as well as an opposition to it. Joe Starks's funeral is narrated as a pompous event encompassing relevant rituals of the black community; however, Janie is only physically juxtaposed, hiding behind her veil, which seems "like a wall of stone and steel [. . .] [while] the funeral was going on outside" (84). Overlapping spatialities are emphasized by the fact that Janie is experiencing inner revitalization: "Weeping and wailing outside. Inside the expensive black folds were resurrection and life" (84). Vivid inner life enabled by forced outsiderness imposed on her by both her deceased husband and the black community can nevertheless have only limited external realization up to the Eatonville period. The ritual interface between community and individual vanishes radically when Janie's third husband, Tea Cake, dies. Dramatically Janie disregards custom and violates the boundaries of the official sacred. The inside gains ground over the external as Janie transforms the site of the funeral for the time being. In sharp contrast to the previous funeral she is wearing "no expensive veils and robes [. . .] this time" (180), but her simple overalls. Whereas Starks's funeral is presented as pompous with Janie, a grieving prop to fulfill formalities as required by his status in the community; Tea Cake's is narrated in a personal tone with Janie, who breaks through social customs with her honest mourning: "She was too busy feeling grief to dress like grief" (180). Thus the funeral in the muck verifies Hurston's general concept of the muck: it represents the inversion of middle class black social space and claims to be the space in a religious sense, in which the individual can attain fullness of selfrealization and selfrevelation.

In an anthropological context, *Their Eyes* can be seen as an initiation narrative (or an immersion narrative to use Stepto's term), in which the final scene of the muck represents the ultimate liminal place of simultaneous purification and becoming. Not only does Janie recount Phoeby her journey as a novice—as Hurston also witnessed novices' accounts before their becoming full members of the religio-cultural community; but the narrative also shows the structure of visions. It narrates Janie's trials and tribulations through three marriages representing the threefold evolving of visions. Dolan Hubbard identifies these three stages as "spiritual orientation," "richness and diversity of the styles of life in the black community," and "the blues impulse" (par. 5). Though, from the point of view of gender, the three husbands represent Janie's development of a female subjectivity, the three stages also lead her toward both a broader contextualization of the self in the black community as her immersion in the open, indefinite space of the black Everglades indicates, and a cosmological understanding of herself.

The trope of the hurricane heightens the symbolic relevance of Janie's visionary journey. Hurston fictionally reworked probably the events of the Okeechobee Hurricane that hit the region in 1928, causing the flooding of Lake Okeechobee and the subsequent death of more than a thousand predominantly migrant black workers then buried in mass graves (see Steinberg 61).

Several critics approach the image of the hurricane through the race discourse. For Erik D. Curren the hurricane represents "a switch from optimistic quest to gothic horror" within a master-slave dialectic (par. 5). On a more permissive note, though, but still within the race discourse, Hubbard positions this religious experience in the racial climate of contemporary America:

> The storm in this, Janie's last movement toward the horizon, symbolizes the struggle the corporate black community has to come to terms with in the oppressor's negation of its image. Out of this negation, the mythic consciousness seeks a new beginning in the future by imagining an original beginning. The social implications of this religious experience enable the oppressed community to dehistoricize the oppressor's hegemonic dominance. Metaphorically, the phrase their eyes were watching God means the creation of a new form of humanity—one that is no longer based on the master-slave dialectic. (par. 58)

While Hubbard touches upon a necessary implication of Janie's religious experience, he fails to break out of the vicious circle of racial projection. On a similar note Richard M. Merelman understands cultural projection as "the conscious or unconscious effort by a social group and its allies to place new images of itself before other social groups, and before the general public" (3). But this kind of projection maintains the focus of the other, thereby unable to perform as a tool of authentication that Hubbard insists on. In fact, this interpretation of the hurricane reiterates racial stereotypes, that is, Uncle Tomism, which posits the African American subject as irreparably religious, otherworldly, and docile—a conceptualization in stark contrast to Hurston's evaluation of religion as mentioned at the beginning of this essay. Hubbard misses the point by focusing on African American racial identity in a social space, the muck, which proves pluralistic and polyphonic before the hurricane, exhibiting "non-polarized social-natural relations" (Stein 478). The new/original beginning for Janie is not a matter of the racial self, but one of contextualization (the prime vehicle of which constitutes storytelling).

Racial criticism misses the richness of Hurston's dynamic trickster philosophy. So while the racial dialectic also appears in the hurricane scene, it may simply mark polyphonic thinking on Hurston's part. Therefore the separation of Christianity and African American folk religious phenomena, Curren urges, cannot hold even from an anthropological point of view (*see* Mintz and Price), but in addition is debunked in Hurston's work because of the anthropologically justified syncretism of different religious spaces Hurston implements in her fiction on the basis of her own research. Examples in *Jonah's* include the myriads of Africanisms in the black church and deacon Harris's voodoo worshipping (147).

Beyond dramatically narrating an actual disaster, the hurricane depicts symbolically Janie's reemergence in the tripartite initiation narrative. Similarly to Job, who undergoes immense suffering as he loses family, fortune, and wealth, and who is tempted by unfeeling friends to abandon his faith, Janie, too, loses the ideal life in the Everglades in a tormenting series of events. In his agony looking for answers, Job confronts God, who speaks to him "out of a storm" (NIV)/ "out of the whirlwind" (KJV) in Job 38. Catherine Keller identifies in the story of Job the "Genesis creation narrative [. . .] as its primary intertext" (124)—a claim supported by God's monologue: "Who shut up the sea behind doors when it burst forth from the womb, when I made the clouds its garment and wrapped it in thick darkness" (Job 38:8-9). Keller argues that the depiction of the universe goes beyond simply stating God's omnipotence (129) to portray "the wild spirit of creation" in which "the sea's ferocity is portrayed as the agitation of an infant that requires boundaries for its own protection-not just for the safety of the earth" (130). Overriding traditional conceptualizations of light versus dark as good versus evil, Keller in her subsequent Bakhtinian analysis proposes that "[i]t is as if the shift from legal to cosmogonic discourse delegalized and deprivatized Job's questions. They entered the intense proximity of the *comic* plane—just as they opened into the bottomless expanse of *cosmic* space" (Keller 139). Janie encounters the same Jobian cosmological experience when Janie makes the confession that "Ah wuz fumblin' round and God opened de door" (151), the storm hits with a symbolic "triple fury," and she finds herself in the midst of a vortex widening the horizon to the open space of the Everglades. Being caught up in the vortex metaphorically represents Janie's encounter with the divine; more specifically, like Job has a final encounter with God and is cleansed, whereby he acknowledges God's supremacy and his own human condition ("My ears had heard of you but now my eyes have seen you. Therefore I despise myself and repent in dust and ashes" [Job 42: 5-6]), Janie, too, becomes aware of her condition in relation to the universe on the level of religious experience enshrined in her vision as well as on a ritual level in relation to the black sacred cosmos, and is thus symbolically purified.

What happens in the hurricane presents a necessary step in the ritual process, "[initiation] is a fundamental existential experience because through it a man becomes able to assume his mode of being in its entirety" (Eliade *Rites and Symbols* 3). In Janie's storytelling of her conversion vision, the hurricane symbolizes coming through religion in two ways: a) Janie's maturation becomes complete in finishing her ritual journey; b) this passing the threshold is ritually expressed through the act of storytelling, whereby Janie becomes contextualized in social space in her own right—that is, her ability to voice an authentic story confirms her subjectivity in the community.

As Keller identifies an element of the comic in Job, the comic is also present in the hurricane scene. Motor Boat, a friend of Janie and Tea Cake's, chooses not to flee from the flood but to go upstairs and sleep. After the hurricane Tea Cake reports that "Heah we nelly kill our fool selves runnin' way from danger and him lay up dere and sleep and float on off" (165). Motor Boat, whose name indicates the irony, survives while in a surrealistic scene Janie and Tea Cake are fighting for their lives on the back of a mule against a rabid dog. The flood lulls Motor Boat into sweet sleep in the midst of mass deaths.

Understanding the scope of her journey and return to Eatonville equals mapping both geographically and spiritually the horizon of black (sacred) space, and her ability to voice her experience marks her embededness in it, that is, similarly to her overalls, presents a "proof of her new baptism" (Dixon 94). Maturation and embededness ring through her voice as she begins revealing her ritual journey with the wisdom of elders: "So t'ain't no use in me telling you somethin' unless Ah give you de understandin' to go 'long wid it. Unless you see de fur, a mink skin ain't no different from coon hide" (7). In a sense Janie takes on a position much like Nanny's (structurally, but unlike Nanny's materialistic philosophy). Nanny gives Janie "de text" (16), "a sermonic monologue" (Hubbard par. 13), not only as a grandmother, but as an elder in the community who shares "motherwit" with Janie.

Motherwit derives from African American cosmology and denotes folk wisdom. Former slave Francis Lewis formulates a definition of motherwit as— "Well, ... [motherwit] is like this: I got a wit to teach me what's wrong. I got a wit to not make me a mischief-maker. I got a wit to keep people's trusts" (Clayton 159)—that appears to be general common sense (see Logan), reflecting also the ex-slave Nanny's spirituality. However, a) motherwit comprises the group-specific expression of experiences regarding race, gender, and class, inducing group-specific normative action; and b) motherwit also reflects African American cosmological thinking, representing a signifier of the African American community, but often understood as "the collective body of female wisdom" (Carr-Hamilton 72).

Delores S. Williams reasserts this approach when writing about the relation between African American women and Hagar, parallels the two fates as to oppression and exploitation by both males and other females. She describes Hagar's story in the Bible as womanist God-talk ("theology") to show that minority women are not forlorn by God despite the defocusing strategies of mainstream discourses. In connecting this religious experience to wilderness experience, Williams renders it, in fact, parallel and complementary individuation. As early as in her marriage with Starks, Janie makes a confession similar to Hagar' story. When Starks mocks women, Janie openly comes to the defense of women: "sometimes God gits familiar wid us womenfolks too and talks His inside business" (70). She thereby claims an up-to-that-point invisible discourse and foregrounds it. Her testimony stands in sharp contrast to the mule's funeral, which can be seen as a trampling on Janie's vision in a surrealistic scene because it identifies black women as "nature incarnate–as 'donkeys' created for nothing more than brute labor and sexual service" (Stein 467), but also as an inverted "steal away" act that justifies Janie morally. In the hurricane scene, "their eyes were watching God" does not refer to a turn away from a bipolar social world, but symbolizes hope in God; that is, a turn toward black sacred space. It also demonstrates the presence of the divine, which shows God's self-revelation before Janie and simultaneous assurance of divine comfort in a time of trial and tribulation.

The initiating hurricane thus marks the completion of Janie's individuation, as testified to her final allegoric act: "Here was peace. She pulled in her horizon like a great fish-net. Pulled it from around the waist of the world and draped it over her shoulder. So much of life in its meshes! She called in her soul to come and see" (184). The post-initiation phase in the narrative condenses the richness of Janie's inner life that she boils down from her experiences; it provides her with integrity as well as endows her with the knowledge, or motherwit of the elders. The muck experience completed by the hurricane scene marks the final move "from the sweltering depths of a culture's swampland to a reconquered, redefined place in the home" (Dixon 87), whereby the depths adheres to religious depth and the redefined home to religious emergence. The life- and self-affirming act presents a parallel with Hurston's ars poetica discussed at the beginning of this essay. Similarly to Janie, Hurston, too, seems to look back at her life in the last chapters of *Dust Tracks* and confirms that "Life, as it is, does not frighten me, since I have made my peace with the universe as I find it, and bow to its laws" (278).[29]

In Hurston's cultural cosmos the liminal places as both antipictures and building blocks of black Christianity provide the cultural binary within the black sacred cosmos in a rather structuralist way—a circumstance that has its own importance. In Hurston's cultural teleology black cultural space proves heteronomy and totality, from where the African American subject can emerge, yet Hurston authenticates her cultural space as an autonomous entity with the help of liminal places. In/of Hurston's religio-cultural space liminality or transition can be considered the general and "permanent condition" (Turner 107) of African Americans, ascertaining cultural dynamics through hybridization. Furthermore, such a treatment of space reveals Hurston's cultural politics: by suturing the sacred into the cultural to such an extent, she does establish a mythic universe based on repeatability, much as Eliade approaches sacred time: "Sacred time [. . .] appears under the paradoxical aspect of a circular time, reversible and recoverable, a sort of mythical present that is periodically reintegrated by means of rites" (70). This method does not, in the first place, reflect fixity, but rather mirrors Hurston's, the anthropologist's, understanding of and experience with culture, as well as, specifically, the organic diversity of African American culture in her books. To quote Eliade again "through the repetition, the *reactualization*, of the traditional rites, the entire community is regenerated" (*Rites and Symbols* 4). Thus Hurston's apparently mythic universe serves to revitalize African American culture and identity by remotivating the cultural plethora.

---

[29] Hurston's evaluation of her life in her concluding chapter is remarkably reminiscent of Janie's concluding phase. When Hurston confesses that "I have been in Sorrow's kitchen and licked out all the pots. Then I have stood on the peaky mountain wrappen in rainbows, with a harp and a sword in my hands" (280), she claims a similar, parallel evaluation of her own life.

6. Gendered Space: Transparent Space, Female Social Space, and the Production of the Female Body

6.1. Masculine Social Space as Transparent Space

> Ships at a distance have every man's wish on board. For some they come in with the tide. For others they sail forever on the horizon, never out of sight, never landing until the Watcher turns his eyes away in resignation, his dreams mocked to death by Time. That is the life of men.
>
> Now, women forget everything they don't want to remember, and remember everything they don't want to forget. The dream is the truth. Then they act and do things accordingly. (*Their Eyes* 1)

Besides the race stratum, it is the stratum of gender, which determines the identity and social positioning of black women in Barbara Johnson's tetrapolar structure. Cultural determinism appears therefore in the fact that Hurston's females are positioned in gendered space. In this chapter I will examine places in which women are incarcerated: in particular, my focus centers on spatial settings to explore how the female body is produced in hegemonic masculine social space, as well as the dynamics of female place construction, that is, how women in Hurston's fiction retain subjectivity through the counterhegemonic activity of shaping their own places and social spaces and obtain integration in a socio-cultural context.

Female place-construction shows female spatiality, hence an always already female subjectivity—even though conditioned by broader contexts such as social space—that denotes a spatial imagination independent of its materialization. The epigraph indicates that the narrator of *Their Eyes* establishes a spatiality preceding place-construction and, indeed, "being-in-the-world" for Hurston's women is often not material. Truth experienced by her women in their dreams, visions; and, in general, mentally and spiritually provides the basis for the exploration of space. Memory offers thus both a spatiality of subjectivity and a challenge to the dominant (masculine) social space (Singh 6).

In this way, the epigraph establishes a dialectics of social space, in which:

> The movement in and out of gender [. . .] is a movement between the (represented) discursive space of the positions available by hegemonic discourses and the space-off, the elsewhere, of those discourses: those other spaces both discursive and social that exist [. . .] in the margins [. . .]. These two kinds of spaces [. . .] coexist concurrently and in contradiction. The movement between them [. . .] is the tension of contradiction, multiplicity, and heteronomy. (De Lauretis 26)

The dynamic movement of female subjects becomes conspicuous in oppressive social spaces in which Hurston's female characters are not allowed to construct their genuine places and are forced to turn toward alternative solutions such as female communal spaces or to individual female places.

It is the former, oppressive social space that shapes the focus of the present subchapter. Oppressive space is "transparent space" (Rose 40)—a term I borrow from feminist geographers to refer to masculine social space that is viewed by these thinkers as public and hegemonic. In this social space the female body has a symbolic value as determined by patriarchal society. The symbolic/metaphorical (Rose 58) body is what Susan Bordo calls the "intelligible body" that "includes [. . .] our cultural conceptions of the body," such as norms, influencing the implementation of positioning of women in transparent social space as "useful bodies" (*Unbearable Weight* 181), or "docile bodies" in Foucauldian coinage (see *Discipline and Punish*). While it is customary to speak, concerning such contexts, of the public/private divide, the latter realm cannot be regarded autonomous space, in other words, a place constructed by women; instead, it marks exclusion from public social space and the body politics of positioning as well as of the inscription of "normalcy" on the body. Hurston's women are often positioned in the private—most prominently: kitchens, bedrooms, back porches, and back yards; and rarely in the public—where they are marginalized and alienated. These women are thus ascribed to inflexible places, where, under the male gaze, they become immobile. Outside the home and masculine social space they evolve into "nomads" (to use Rosi Bradiotti's term) in the sense that they are excluded and placeless, yet mobile.

In the feminist discourse of space, transparent space denotes masculine space, which is conceptualized as homogeneous and uncontested. It represents the social construction of masculinity: it is seen as public (as opposed to private femininity), hegemonic, and heterosexual (see Hanson and Pratt); as well as it internalizes in the male subject the connectedness of masculinity to such notions as the outside, the official, the rational, the elevated (Bourdieu, *Férfiuralom* 38), or the representative (56). Transparency refers to order, that is, control and domination, in the first place. Certainly, it has consequences for men as much it does for women. As Bourdieu points out, masculinity must be understood in terms of relationality as it is constructed within a male collectivity (with respect to other men) and in spite of women (*Férfiuralom* 62). The male subject is placed in a social space, in which he is endowed with expectations both enabling and limiting. It is clear that transparency describes a regulatory (or intelligible as Bordo would have it) framework; but it cannot deny the multiplicity of masculinity as the example of Tea Cake in *Their Eyes* also proves. Judith Butler too criticizes the idea of a "universal patriarchy," arguing for the diversity of cultural background in which it appears ("Subjects of Sex" 3), and Miklós

Hadas calls attention to the deconstruction of hegemonic masculinity by insisting on its multiplicity (40). On the one hand, transparent space becomes an oppressive framework if it can handle inner disruptions. As Lefebvre insists, "Space assumes a regulatory role when and to the extent that contradictions—including contradictions of space itself—are resolved" (420). On the other hand, the assumed multiplicity of masculine space establishes that males can appear in oppressed positions in masculine social space as well as women, while, for the latter, marginalized positions are presupposed.

For Hurston's women transparent masculine space effects exclusion, surveillance, and situatedness in terms of work, time, and place (Bourdieu, *Férfiuralom* 17-18). The threefold stratification differentiating the masculine and the feminine is connected through praxis, which constitutes the discursive production of femininity in Hurston's works. More specifically, Hurston's socio-cultural space is constructed around the public/private divide, which regulates the positioning of her female characters, in the first place, by the assignment of places, domestic work, and the limitation on mobility. Hurston establishes that in transparent masculine social space of this socio-cultural space women are placed in the private sphere of social space, or else they appear in a marginalized position in masculine (public) places. Both types of enclosed places detectable in these works present women in an environment in which they are socialized into gender through "the repeated stylization of the body" (Butler, "Subjects of Sex" 33) under the regulatory male gaze.

Female places in masculine social space are, thus, gendered places, where women are defined and positioned *within*—in enclosed places, which render them immobile, out of sight, and voiceless. Their position is foregrounded in both novels: 1) in *Jonah's Gourd Vine* (essentially the fictionalization of Hurston's family history evolving around a male protagonist) our first encounter of Lucy places her within the fences of the school garden, and, with the passing of time, her case becomes worse in the sense that we find her mostly in the bedroom; 2) in *Their Eyes Were Watching God* the initial two stages of Janie's evolution mark the domination of enclosed places: the kitchen at Logan Killicks's place and Jodie Starks's big, white house and his store.

The comparison between Janie's conception of Killicks's house exemplifies well what enclosed places mean for Hurston's women. This is valid despite the fact that only scarce number of objects describe the spatial setting of Killicks's lower class house, as opposed, for example, to Jodie Starks's big white house belonging to the middle class. In the case of the former, the location of the place and the discursive maneuver of positioning the female body, which also lacks supportive props—the subjective rendering of objects—are indicative of the nature of place.

In Nanny's materialistic understanding, which is a prime example of how power produces knowledge and perpetuates appropriate, normalized behavior—

also to promote action in favor of the patriarchal order—as well as generates a subject position in masculine social space: to be situated in a man's house implies protection in a hostile masculine world, in which women, nevertheless, "uh pullin' and uh haulin' and sweatin' and doin' from can't see in de mornin' till can't see at night" (22). Despite Nanny's intentions, her remark points to a disruption in her argument: the time span in this reference establishes a cultural regulation between time and social space in that the overwhelming presence of the latter is prohibiting to female privacy, in which gendered job roles are advocated. In Nanny's view, security, or, rather, social acceptance in masculine transparent space is obtained for Janie through the integration in gendered places such as Killicks's house. Gendered socialization becomes palpable in her narrative, when she explains the importance of marriage to Janie: "De thought uh you bein' kicked around from pillar tuh post is a hurtin' thing" (15); and then: "Ah can't die easy thinkin' maybe de menfolks white or black is makin' a spit cup outa you" (19). Nanny denies any possibility of selffulfillment (even though her vision used to include for her daughter, who was then seduced by a [male] teacher, to become a teacher—a considerable upward movement on the social ladder for her), the relevance of Janie's vision under the pear tree; and she accepts gendered places as the negotiated site of identity formation. Her conceptualization of a home parallels Mona Domosh's understanding of the home, which, for her, represents "a site of confirming gender and sexual identities" (277). Indeed, Nanny views the home as the site of initiation into womanhood, but that can, in fact, be equated with entering the (reproductive) labor market of the household. Initiation refers here to discipline and the sense of integration signifies the production of knowledge that is, for example, revealed in "the internalized patriarchal standard" (Bartky 77) of accepting marital abuse. This becomes palpable when Janie asks Nanny for advice a short time after the wedding: "Lawd, Ah know dat grass-gut, liver-lipted nigger ain't done took and beat mah baby *already*!" (21, emphasis added).

In *Jonah's*, the harsh social environment of the working class places John's mother, Amy, in a similar position to Nanny and Janie at this point. Hurston conceptualizes this character too as restricted to the household. However, Amy's position is different from theirs since she is surrounded by the protecting shield of her sons against their stepfather, Ned. In a scene, for example, when Ned whips and beats Amy, she "wheel[s] to fight" (8), and John comes to her aid. In this sense, her status is ambiguous in masculine transparent space: while she is located in the home (the reproduction site of social space), exposed to the violence of her husband, and her existence can well be characterized by immobility, whereby the "local labor market" makes her oscillate between house and field, she is granted a well-established, empowering space as a mother, and also a voice in protection for her sons. The legitimation of Amy's position in the house becomes ostentatious before the fighting, when "[t]he clash and frenzy in the air was almost visible" (7), precipitating the divisions between the opposing parties in the social space of the home; and "Ned stood up and shuffled toward the door" (7), whereby he unknowingly accepts that "the house is women's spatial domain" (Pellow 162). Despite Amy's firm identification with the house, which means security, but it also imposes on her limiting anchorage (which is why she cannot leave with John) and reveals thus a socially constructed identity, which is void of selffulfillment. The description of the place echoes Nanny's life in *Their Eyes*, when Amy, after saying good-bye to his son in the open, where "For a minute she had felt free and flighty" (12), she returned to the house "across the barren hard clay yard" (12). The barrenness of the working class female life parallels Nanny's barren tree-like statue and indicates the devastation of her life simultaneously.

Both Amy's and Nanny's narratives prove the presence of the knowledge-producing mechanism of masculine and racial power, but this mechanism also leaves its imprints on their body. As Foucault claims, "the social body is the effect [. . .] of the materiality of power operating on the very bodies of individuals" ("Body/Power" 55). Power can be pinpointed in "the *constitution* of the very materiality of the subject" (Butler, *Bodies that Matter* 34)—in its physicality and positionality, as well as in the politics of mobility (Law 583). This refers to the discourse of the body; but, as Butler argues, places have materiality too inasmuch they are instruments and vehicles of power, that is, they are "*invested with power*" (Butler, *Bodies that Matter* 34). More precisely, "[t]he whole of (social) space proceeds from the body, even though it so metamorphoses the body that it may forget it altogether—even though it may separate itself so radically from the body as to kill it" (Lefebvre 405). Spatial discourses involve, therefore, the interrelation of both body, itself "concreteness and concrete (and limiting) *location*" (Bordo, *Twilight Zones* 185), and space.

In Nanny's case, the home has the function of mediating the discursive acts of regulating the body regarding "its very forces and operations, the economy and efficiency of its movements" and the proliferation of "the utility of the body" (Bartky 61, 62). Apart from the situatedness of Nanny's working class, female body, which is viewed as an old tree "torn away by storm" and that "no longer mattered" (*Their Eyes* 12), the engendering of the body is insufficiently described. One can induce Hurston's concept of working class homes and the female body in these places, for instance, on the basis of her short story, "Sweat." Delia's home parallels Killicks's place and Amy's home; and Delia's description, who is a washwoman (that is, in the same class as Janie at this point of her development), represents what Amy has become and what Janie might have become. As it is narrated, "her knotty, muscled limbs, her harsh knuckly hands" (957) have come to characterize her work-worn body that stands in sharp contrast (as in Janie's case) with the garden of selfplanted trees and flowers. The radical geography of Delia's alienation can be pinpointed on

Delia's body, which signifies, in Lefebvre's mode, the separation of the body and space, as well as it bears the marks of the regulatory function of space.

The two occasions, when Janie is imparted a lecture at this stage, occur in Nanny's bedroom and in Mrs. Washburn's kitchen, with Nanny preparing biscuits—gendered places for women within the house. At these places Janie is socialized into the acceptance of her gender roles by Nanny's narrative. It takes place inside houses and is conducted by a woman, which proves how gender has grown to "congeal over time to produce the appearance of substance of a natural sort of being" (Butler, "Subjects of Sex" 33) in women for it to become selfperpetuating. As it is narrated: "she [Janie] extended herself outside of her dream and went inside the house. That was the end of her childhood" (12). Nanny and the spatial discourse of the places associated with her fulfill power-related functions to incorporate Janie into the masculine order. Spatial anchorage of Janie's vision outside the built environment forms a contrast with Nanny's house, which heightens Nanny's malfunction as a "spiritual mentor" or "spiritual mother" (Alonzo Johnson, "Pray's House Spirit" 29), and renders Nanny's house a socio-spatial fixation, and her sense of place akin to Killicks's place.

Contrary to Janie's expectations ("Ah wants things sweet wid mah marriage lak when you sit under a pear tree and think" [23]), her marriage to Logan Killicks turns out to be a material treatise, an undesired *job* with clearly defined gender roles emplaced in definite spheres of the house. Initially, Janie finds there not sweetness, but a "lonesome place like a stump in the middle of the woods where nobody had ever been" (20), a house "absent of flavor" (21). The strong contrast between the metaphors of a stump defocalized by the immensity of the woods and the trope of the visionary blossoming pear tree, which centers place around itself and heightens the sense of Janie's alienation. Establishing a nature/culture binary, Michael Awkward draws a parallel between Genesis and Janie's "natural education" in the "ahistorical backyard," where Janie is presented as a "prelapsarian, precultural human being" (19) and a prophetess. Conversely, Killicks's house proves to be a place of incarceration here too as Janie experiences it at Nanny's. It crowds in on her. Nevertheless, accepting temporarily the gender roles signified by the framework of the kitchen, she still maintains her vision and tries to find validification of her dream revelation under the pear tree, but to no avail. The lack of the description of the inner structuring of Killicks's house, apart from the visible separation of gender roles, establishes this place for Janie as empty, void of personal significance, and, therefore, oppressive. It "signif[ies] only absence and death" (25). In fact, the vigorous Janie with the cornmeal dough positioned in the kitchen is threatened to become predictably the younger version of Nanny with the bread board as she appears in Mrs. Washburn's kitchen, which is in accordance with Nanny's materialistic vision for Janie.

A dual change in the spatial setting, denoting opposing directions, appears within a short time when Killicks begins to put pressure on Janie to extend her sphere of work beyond the walls of the kitchen. Fulfilling Nanny's foreshadowing statement ("He's kissin' yo' foot and 'tain't in uh man tuh kiss foot long. [. . .] when dey got to bow down tuh love, dey soon straightens up" [22]), Killicks leaves for Lake City to buy her a mule to plow with, explaining later that "Tain't no use in fooling round in dat kitchen all day long" (30). At the same time, however, Janie resists this development when, in her rhetoric, she relies on the given division of gender roles spatially established to prevent the completion of her objectification: "Youse in yo' place and Ah'm in mine" (30). Simultaneously, she makes a marked move out of the kitchen, whereby she refuses the extended identification with the place and her assigned role within it. She goes to the barn to work—to "a place in the yard where she could see the road" (26).

Lucy in *Jonah's* has an even more confined space in Alabama. She is locked into the cycle of reproduction that literally relegates her to bed. Her physical enslavement as a breeder is also symbolically reified, since the wedding bed is a gift from Alf Pearson, the white (slave) owner of the place. The bed thus symbolizes the continuation of antebellum slavery in the case of free black women, and frameworks "normative expectations of the gendered body" (Park 213). She is always presented in bed in her marriage both in Alabama and in Eatonville, Florida, where she reaches a middle class status on the side of her husband. The metaphor of the bed signifies disability and social marginalization that really becomes powerful as against the promiscuous behavior of John, who is seldom presented in the home, but whose figure is connected to superior physical power and agency. Lucy's deprivation reaches its climactic point when her brother, Bud, takes away her wedding bed, on which she has come to depend despite its regulatory character: "Lucy was crumpled in a little dark ball in the centre of the deep mound of feathers" (91). The contrast between her broken stature and the nest-like image parallels the demolition of Janie's vision.

Much as Eatonville is presented as the setting of possible social upheaval in both novels for men and for their women, the constraint of class only adds to a sharpened maintenance of gender differences and the representation of gender remains also inscribed in places. Starks and, as a satellite entity, Janie stand on "high ground," which fulfills Nanny's expectations for Janie to be established in the middle class. Hemenway points out that the vertical metaphor of "high" Nanny uses, and which is also induced by Starks, proves how the notion of classism institutionalized by whites in blacks is misleading Hurston's African American community (237). However, Orvar Löfgren's argument concerning the differences between working and middle class home-making does not pertain to a mostly agrarian black community setting, even if the fundamental conceptions of men as "homo economicus" and of women as "femina domestica" (147) are identical. Whereas home for men is a "place of retreat and rest" (Löfgren 146), Hurston shows that middle class women remain captive to working class gender conceptions. So, for example, Starks, relying on an ambiguous class argument, forbids Janie to make speeches on the porch on story-telling occasions because, as "uh big woman" (43), she is supposed to class off: "Ah can't see what uh woman uh yo' stability would want tuh be treasurin' all dat gum-grease from folks dat don't even own de house dey sleep in" (51). The view of the female body reflects white Christian concepts of mythologized female morality Starks has absorbed from Southern (aristocratic) plantation culture, but it functions more like an ideological weapon in his hand to exhibit class power by being chivalric and protective, yet, in fact, demonstrating control over Janie. Women in Hurston's masculine world are ascribed a materialistic and domestic (labor), as well as a symbolic function, but they do not fulfill the symbolic function of intimacy and homeliness (Löfgren 147-48) that marks middle class female roles of the time, at least on an ideological level.

Similarly to Janie's regulation via spatial tactics, that is, through place and body, and through language, Lucy is subjected to the same tactics of power including the constraint of class. The change in Lucy's class position in Eatonville does not change her positionality, either—she remains tied to the domestic sphere, and, most of all, to the bedroom. Separated from her family in Alabama, although also separated from a directly white environment, her social isolation and subjection become even more visible as she never enters the all important porch of the store—the primary form of masculine public space in Eatonville. When, for example, an innocent joke is made on the porch that Lucy might leave the otherwise unfaithful John, he goes home, takes his Winchester into the bedroom, and threatens Lucy that "Ahm de first wid you, and Ah mean tuh be de last [. . .] if you ever start out de door tuh leave me, you'll never make it tuh de gate" (110-1). John proves his dominance over Lucy's small, frail body—an act not only to serve the purpose of discipline, but also to verify his masculinity for John, both before himself and within the male community. As it is narrated, "he held Lucy tightly and thought pityingly of other men" (111). Throughout the novel Lucy remains locked in this position, in the shadow of her husband, and seems to have less mobility and even less voice than Janie in *Their Eyes*. Only on her death bed does she raise her voice once to complain about his lover, Hattie, for which John hits her. Lucy's social marginalization and debasement are even more striking, because Lucy's guidance from the background enables him to accomplish a career also expressed by the porch, when Mayor Moseley calls him "uh wife-made man" (113).

As mentioned above, beyond the construction of masculinity in opposition to femininity, the relational aspect of masculine space requires the validation of masculinity before other males. So in interpreting Addison Gayle, Jr's argument that "the black man's route to manhood lay in the exploitation of black women" (39), it becomes conspicuous that his statement does not only refer to labor or marital abuse, but to games directed at defeat and precedence regarding both men and women (Hadas 34). When people gather on the porch, Starks finds a way to send Janie in the store, an act he takes pleasure in (51), disregarding Janie's preferences, in order to demonstrate a higher class and gender status as a male before other males. John's treatment of Lucy as shown above confirms this thesis. The negotiation of masculine identity is mostly conducted in public spaces, in concert with other males.

In Eatonville the discursive production of femininity appears spatially, in the first place, in both novels, through place and the structuring of place; even when the docilicization of the female body evolves often through the performativity of language. In fact, language occupies a significant role in Janie's Eatonville experience, but language and space complement each other. In Janie's case, they form two conspicuous functions of regulation. Language (or speech) is both situated in space (and often time); e.g., as in the case of evening porch talks, and it is the constitutive element of the Eatonville socio-cultural space. It emplaces Janie in masculine social space, and place provides for the maintenance of this position. Furthermore, in Eatonville agency is assigned to language (voice), and, by the same token, language constructs place. Joe Starks speaks Eatonville, the initially "scant dozen of shame-faced houses" (32), into being by voicing his vision. He first calls for a committee, the nuclear social space of the settlement, which gradually increases through the deployment of a post office/store, his house, and the houses of newcomers. His porch remains the "meetin' place fuh de town" (38), the centre of Eatonville, where story telling, "playin' the dozens," and so on, prove to be the centripetal forces in the community.

Conversely, Starks's new house takes up a regulatory function also for the town as the town becomes "servants' quarters surrounding the 'big house'" (44). Starks, in fact, personifies white power structure in black Eatonville. Since he has been trained under whites, Starks has absorbed their tactics of power, enabling him to build up a plantation structure around his "gloaty, sparkly white" (44) house, which renders him a vehicle of white regulatory power within a broader racial social space. Once time Starks runs a man off the place and the town denounces him as a white slave-master: "He loves obedience out of everybody under de sound of his voice" (46).

The contrast between speech and silence codifies social hierarchy, which is paralleled by the contrast of visibility and invisibility (the public/private divide) to accompany Janie's mode of dwelling throughout this stage of her development. Already at the beginning of their stay in Eatonville, Starks is presented directly on the porch *talking* to men, while Janie "could be seen through the bedroom window getting settled" (34)—a clear indication of the decentering of the female subject. Janie is shown alone, isolated and muted in closed place, secondary to the public space of the porch. Her fixation in space through language becomes a constant practice of Starks's. This becomes obvious, when Tony Taylor asks Janie to articulate some words on the occasion of opening the new store. Starks does not allow her to speak up publicly: "mah wife don't know nothin' 'bout no speech-makin'. Ah never married her for nothin' lak dat. She's uh woman and her place is in de home" (40-41). His statement echoes Killicks's understanding of women; yet, Janie does not speak up immediately against it as she does at Killicks's place beforehand. Still, the instance marks a turning point in their relationship. As Starks's coarse statement "took the bloom off of things" (41), Janie's social marginalization; but also, from a different angle, her centered position as an objectified satellite entity in a higher class, as the "bell-cow" (39) of Eatonville betrays again the vision of the blossoming pear tree surrounded by the alto chant of bees (10).

The "gloaty, sparkly white" house and the store, both constituents of, what Lefebvre calls "dominant space" (39), alienate Janie, since they squeeze her into role-play that renders her "far away from things and lonely" (*Their Eyes* 44). She becomes an unwilling part of Starks's imitation of white male power structure, which separates her also from the rest of the settlement. Her perception of the place shows that her immediate environment grows to be estranging—partly due to monotony that derives from the fact that she is socialized into this setting without the ability to endow it with personal significance, as only labor and "representation" are required from her. The oppressive context of the house and store does not leave her body unmarked either. By having to wear a head-rag, her female subjectivity is attacked, which—as noted before—debunks the middle class ethos of intimacy and beauty as constituting elements of femininity.

Masculine (public) places appear markedly juxtaposed with the private sphere of social space in Eatonville in *Their Eyes*. The porch functions indeed as "a public alternative to the court" (Joseph 467), but, from a gender perspective, not in the sense Philip Joseph uses it: "a place where manifold conflicting viewpoints and endless qualification take precedence over the arrival at a final verdict" (467). It is true that the porch in the African American context and in Hurston's works represents the capstone of culture, where the value hierarchy of the community is articulated, and where identity within the community is negotiated through, for example, the praxis of games and verbal interaction. Especially, from the point of view of the latter, however, the democratic nature of the porch is questioned. As both Lucy's case, who does not appear on the porch at all, and that of Janie, who is marginalized on the porch, women cannot negotiate an identity there; that is, only gendered identities are interpolated in objectified positions. Janie is thus muted on the porch, and other women are the objects of verbal games such as mock courtships. The porch is also the place, where femininity is verbally constituted in public for Janie. Once Starks rebukes Janie on the porch, "All you got tuh do is mind me" (66); and later: "Somebody got to think for women and chillun and cows. I god, they sho don't think none theirselves" (67). Non-acceptance to the porch-community means the denial of subjectivity and social legitimation, while Janie's public debasement that later evolves also around her body (when Starks grows into the habit of mocking her looks), serves both chastising into gender and the validation of masculinity, as Löfgren puts it in another context, to "help underline the maleness of the man in the public sphere" (148).

The constraint of race shapes another form of masculine public space, which appears in both novels: the courthouse. African Americans, regardless of which gender they belong to, know that "Courthouses were bad luck to colored people" (*Jonah's* 165). The courthouse proves to be a "dispositif" (see Deleuze) that denotes not only legal space which mediates masculine order, but also a regulatory interface, a Lefebvrian representation of space, in white (masculine) power structure. In *Jonah's* there are two instances when the apparatus of the court occupies a central role in the narrative. Both times John is brought before court. There he is judged by whites, while blacks bring charges against him— first, for beating up Lucy's brother, and, later in Eatonville, Hattie (his second wife) wants to divorce him. The court in *Jonah's* is important for two reasons. First, it illustrates a racial context, in which African Americans are forced to allow whites to settle matters that emerge among blacks. As it is reported explicitly: "de laws and de cotehouses and de jail houses all b'longed tuh white folks." (165). Also, as an interface, the court superimposes on the African American community and enforces white values in a top-down manner. The court is presented as an impenetrable wall, at which, instead of negotiation, judgment is passed: "John saw the smirking anticipation on the faces of the lawyers, the Court attendants, the white spectators, and felt as if he had fallen down a foul latrine" (167). The non-differentiating gaze of this white panopticon objectifies John as a bad "loafer" (169), and strips him of his pride, replacing it with shame. Second, from a feminine perspective, Hurston empowers, in striking ways, her female characters in such settings. They become heroines like Lucy, who "thrust[s] her frailty between [John] and trouble" (165). The white court becomes a setting, where black males depend on their women for voice. The court scene shows that, while Hurston maintains the concept of the social marginalization in transparent social space, she also rejects the simplistic male/female binary, and insists on the interdependence of black men and black women within a broader white space.

Furthermore, Hurston uses the image of the court to visualize, perhaps, ironically white (female) patronage for black women in face of the African American community. In her career as both a writer and an anthropologist, she had to rely on white patronage—most notably, on her Godmother, Mrs. Mason

(Hemenway 108), while it happened several times that she was confronted by hostility from the black community during her field trips and from black intellectuals who criticized her writing. Janie in *Their Eyes* raises her voice in public in a courtroom the first time, when she is charged of murdering her husband, Tea Cake. The act of telling her story is a testimony of her newly acquired selfconsciousness. The acquittal by the white court sanctions Janie's new consciousness in opposition to the black community. In fact, the black community is marginalized in the courtroom as "colored people [were] standing up in the back of the courtroom [. . .] packed like a case of celery" (176), and they are not allowed to testify before the court. Despite Hurston's love of her own people, she appears utterly critical of them when she calls them an "anonymous herd" (177), while she is sympathetic toward white women.

The image of the court proves to be a powerful metaphor in both major novels by Hurston, where it emerges at decisive moments of the narratives. In the everyday lives of Hurston's female protagonists, however, two metaphors haunt in enclosed spaces. The spatial metaphor of contrast of the ("big") road serves as an important trope for Hurston to define the location of enclosed places. It heightens the contrast between women's situatedness and the seeming unboundedness of the other-than-private sphere. Houses—more importantly: porches—are built on roads (usually on the main road of the settlement), where public and communal events take place. So in Eatonville every evening is "the time for sitting on porches beside the road" (1), where the porch constitutes a genuine cultural space. Furthermore, houses built on the main road also lend status to them in the eyes of the community. Nanny, for example, tries to convince Janie to marry Logan Killicks by arguing that he "Got a house bought and paid for and sixty acres uh land right on de big road [. . .]! Dat's de very prong all us black women gits hung on" (22). For Hurston's important women the big road has thus a dual role. On the one hand, it embodies masculine social space marked by mobility as well as agency, where only men appear; and as a contrast it refers back to female rootedness in closed place. More specifically, the big road for women depicts limited social mobility and marginalization in gendered space. On the other, the roads, beyond representing a mere token of possible escape, metaphorize the horizon for these women. It is reported of Janie that "she began to stand around the gate and expect things" (23) at Killicks's place, and remaining inside the fence "she hung over the gate and looked up the road towards way off" (24). The equation of the roads with expectations becomes more concrete when Janie leaves Killicks and finds that "[t]he morning road air was like a new dress" (31). The sensuous description of Janie's renewed hopes shows her outside lived environment and her identification with nature; or, rather, the wilderness, which, in African American terminology, is the counterspace to social space.

Janie's nonidentification with social space is further strengthened through the metaphor of the veil, which reveals an important pattern of oppositionality in Hurston's gendered places that affect the female body directly. Whereas the house serves as the symbol of the extended self (see Clare Cooper), for Hurston's women it becomes detached from the body, becomes oppressive, regulating the body, and the self is transposed into the natural realm, where identification with place can be instituted. This establishes the functional/pragmatic employment of the Cartesian body; that is, the body is deliberately separated from the self. On the one hand, it presents a mode of selfempowerment through the separation of body and mind. As it is reported in the text, [Janie] had an inside and an outside now and suddenly she knew how not to mix them" (68). "The co-presence of two distinct poles" of inside and outside without "their collapse into oneness" (Johnson, "Metaphor" 165) enables Janie to maintain subjectivity and leads to selfempowerment, which is not connected to "verbal assertiveness" in the first place, as Awkward suggests (32). Selfempowerment is connected to Janie's remembrance of her vision of the pear tree, which is place, to her disembodied mind that proves increasingly a well of memories and ideas, and to her identification with place other than Starks's white house. On the other hand, as Awkward insightfully reminds us, Janie rediscovers nature that effects revitalization through "her psychological reincarnation" (28). Sitting under a tree around the store she experiences the refreshing power of the wind, which works "like a drug" and which "reconcile[s] her to things" (*Their Eyes* 73). The renewed identification with a tree provides her with a place on her own, a "space-off" in Lauretis's coinage, where, through an act of transpatiality, she finds peace and acquiescence in her existence.

The surrealistic scene of the burial of Matt Boner's mule in *Their Eyes* sums up powerfully Hurston's view of transparent space. The scene is significant for two reasons regarding transparent space, even though it has been criticized as a disruption of a realistic plot and as an overdone piece of folklore (Hemenway 234). First, it is interpolated in the story as a dense allegory of female fate in masculine space. Nanny's manifesto ("De nigger woman is de mule uh de world" [14]) renders this scene a macabre inversion of Janie's vision of the pear tree. Here Hurston uses the blossoming tree metaphor implicitly—as she does previously, by likening Killicks's house to a stump—to contrast the ideal with limitation. The tree in bloom is contrasted with the mule carcass and the pollinating bees with buzzards. Evoking the "repressive and regulatory structure"[30] (Butler, "Subjects of Sex" 35) of patriarchy, Starks and another man stand on the "distended belly of the mule" (57) to make mocking speeches and,

---

[30] It must be noted that in the context of this reference Butler promotes a view that questions a universal "transcultural notion of patriarchy" (35).

then, the village leaves the mule for the buzzards to devour. Second, on the story level, Starks's denial for Janie to participate in this social event marks a culminating point in her subservience. While the entire town goes to the funeral, she is marginalized socio-spatially, as she has to stay behind in the home: "*you ain't goin' off in all dat mess uh commonness* [. . .] Shet de door behind yuh, Janie" (56-57). The instance also exposes Janie the farthest from her original (envisioned) precultural/natural state. As Hemenway rightly suggests, "the restriction illustrates how she is out of touch with the cadence of nature" (234-35).

Transparent masculine social space thus provides the context for Hurston's women, in which they experience places as "social products" (Soja, *Postmodern Geographies* 126). In the microcosm of places under the male gaze they are exposed to dematerialization. However, it is not only the male gaze that proves subversive for Hurston's women, but also a network of other women.

6.2. Female Social Space

The inner functioning of masculine social space goes with a strategy of power, which crystallizes as female social space. This space bears similar traits to masculine transparent space. The reasons are twofold: a) female social space is structured on similar premises as its masculine counterpart, that is, to maintain the female status quo via subversive power mechanisms; b) the female status quo exists much in relation to masculine transparent space, as a kind of subspace for "reproduction of social relations" (Lefebvre 50), which shows the naturalization of (white) masculine values in the female consciousness, and that female communal "[s]tructures are both the medium and the outcome of social practices" (Parker Pearson and Richards 3). In this way, Hurston's struggle to establish a genuine female space marks also strife against a *female transparent space*.

In both novels the status of transparent female subspace within the masculine conceptualized space (see Lefebvre 38) is easily recognizable. It derives from the traditional and gendered division of labor that ascribes spatially, in the first place, the domestic sphere to women, as well as from the gendered distribution of social roles. It is true that the status of women renders a high degree of social and spatial immobility in these novels; however, it also demarcates a limited space for women, where, in accordance with the rules of masculine transparency, women can acquire a gendered position of power. Furthermore, much like Sartre's practico-inert ensemble this space also effects homogeneity in praxis, that is, in the mediation of masculine power. The limited spatial framework construes a social space with a clear hierarchy along lines of race, gender, and class. Thus, arguably, the female subspace is a dispositif within the larger masculine function: it shapes a power centre for the socialization of women and for the interpolation of gendered identities.

Interestingly, the existence of female social space often suggests the juxtaposition of the two transparent spaces with the apparent exclusion of males from female spaces. From time to time, the relative autonomy of female social space is manifest in both novels. In *Jonah's*, for example, rituals around birth and death enacted by women grants marginal position to males. Similarly, in *Their Eyes* Janie, Nanny, and Mrs. Washburn, the white landlady, shape a community in which men do not appear at all.

The relationship of the two transparent spaces to each other produces a dynamics that is, however, not based on mutuality or reciprocity. Rather, as a subspace, female transparency is complementary, enabling the system to function smoothly, effecting "continuity [and] cohesion" (as I quote Lefebvre [33] in Chapter 2) by the indoctrination of both men and women via the production of knowledge, and, consequently, appropriate social behavior.

The female community displays three spatialities, similar to Mazumdar's stratification of female roles in the case of the Hindu house (161): familial space, ritual space, and communal space. Here I want to concentrate on communal space as I have already elaborated on domestic spaces and already dealt with Hurston's sacred space. Suffice it to say, female ritual space in Hurston's works is largely constructed by birth rituals and death rituals. *Jonah's* offers excellent examples in this regard. Lucy's childbirth is attended by a friend, Pheemy, who, aided by two assistants, "performed the ancient rites" (92). Birth is purified through ritual, but also, in this way, Lucy is taken up by the community "so that no harm could come to [her]" (92). Ritual naturalizes her into and renders her intelligible for the community. As Émile Durkheim points out regarding ritual practice: "[. . .] practices [. . .] unite its adherents in a single moral community [. . .]" (46). However, the ritual is not necessary to support Janie's subjectivity. As Carla L. Peterson notes about communities: "[. . .] women most often entered the space of *communitas* alone and remained isolated within it [. . .]. Indeed, they rarely became part of the communitas but rather maintained an ambiguous insider/outsider status to it" (39). Even more conspicuously, Lucy's death agony shows how ritual seemingly sets her apart from males, yet her wish to be buried as she wants is denied by cultural ritual enacted by women. As much as immersion in a community is conditioned, departure from it is also systematized. The female leader of the ritual concerts the tasks and does not allow Lucy's wishes to be granted. Thus, for example, despite Lucy's explicit desire—"don't let 'em take de pillow from under mah head, and be covering up de clock and de lookin' glass [. . .]" (130)—the women enacting the ritual tasks take away the pillow. In her agony Lucy is silent, but her silence also signifies her lack of control over the events: her bedroom becomes—as Kathleen Komar theorizes enclosed spaces—an "arena of punishment or at least confinement" (91), not at all unlike her experience of masculine transparent space. As a result of spatial practice, Lucy is marginalized even in the centre, and only her eyes reveal her will and her dependence on Isis's selfassertion, when "Isis saw her set eyes fasten on her" (132). Conversely, the fact that Janie is excluded from Starks's sick room and his death agony in the bedroom shows her marginalization, which she, in fact, breaks, by going into the bedroom to reassert herself before Starks. She does so successfully, which is also ritually expressed as she manages to occupy the leading role in the ritual and thereby to reclaim her social role, despite previous neglect: "Come heah people! Jody is dead. Mah husband is gone from me" (83).

The inner structuring of female social space thus enhances appropriate social behavior to a great degree, emerging powerfully in both Nanny's and Mrs. Turner's case. For both these characters assimilation to white masculine values embodies the peak of social upheaval. Neither of these women can imagine an independent woman as a functioning unit of their community. As Kevin Everod Quashie hypothizes African American female subjectivity at one point:

> Black female subjects mostly materialize as figures of difference in someone else's complicated subjectivity [. . .]. In fact, if the intersectionality that binary identity systems make necessary is definitive of Black women's experience of subject, then it seems almost ideologically and theoretically impossible for there to be a Black female essentialism: the subjectivity is too piecemeal, too deployed in something other than itself, too much an afterthought of Black men's or white women's totalization of race or gender. (9)

For both characters female identity is grounded in something other than itself. Nanny's preoccupation with capital shows how gender and class are interwoven for her. Mrs. Turner exemplifies how race and class join to shape the peak of female upward mobility in transparent space. She associates color with refinement: the lighter (that is, closer to white people in complexion) a person is, the higher position s/he deserves in the community. Mrs. Turner's complexion, her pointed nose, her thin lips, her statue, and her brother's straight hair grant her the desired similarity to whites and urge her to "class off" (135). Her selfhatred becomes pronounced: "Ah don't blame de white folks from hatin' em 'cause Ah can't stand 'em mahself" (135). Her nonidentification with and her distancing from the African American community is shown explicitly by her objectifying her people as "them." Her ideology positions her above her people on the basis of the constraint of race: "We oughta lighten up de race" (135). Her dilemma is not to enlighten the workers of the Everglades or to bring about reform, but it verifies her positioning in transparent space and in its female subspace. Not only does she define herself in connection with whites, more specifically, with the white middle class, but, in addition, she does so by defining herself in relation to men. When, for example, a brawl is initiated in her restaurant to reprimand her, she is seeking to rely on her husband "to put a stop to things" (144). In a rather comical way, Hurston reveals that in Mrs. Turner's consciousness power is ultimately connected to masculinity despite what her elitist standoffishness and her ideology-induced speeches would suggest.

The pluralistic nature of the muck cannot coexist with hegemonic discourses presented by Mrs. Turner, so she is driven away; but elsewhere in Georgia, for example, as Emmeline's character proves in *Jonah's*, classism along lines of race and gender is a common practice. Kathy Russel shows that light complexion has been connected to elitism (24) in the African American community, so much so that mulattos formed a "buffer class" (15) between whites and blacks. Light complexion denoted higher status in the racial matrix, but also psychological indoctrination in favor of white values. A simple binary is established thus between the ideal woman of light skin color on the side of a man, reflecting values of (white) male transparent space, and those women who lack any of the outstanding values of these constrains, be it capital, a man, or light complexion.

The strong differentiation along these lines can be noticed as early as childhood. In fact, very similar structures can be detected in children's communities in both novels. In *Their Eyes* Janie tells her friend, Pheoby Watson, how she was different early in her childhood, when she and Nanny were living on Washburn's property:

> Mis' Washburn useter dress me up in all de clothes her gran'chillun didn't need no mo' which wuz better'n whut de rest uh de colored chillum had. And then she useter put hair ribbon on mah head fuh me tuh wear. Dat useter rile Mayrella uh lot. So she would pick at me all de time and put others up tuh do de same. They'd push me'way from de ring plays and make out they couldn't play wid nobody dat lived on premises. (9)

Not only does Hurston establish Janie as an outsider from early on, she also calls attention to the background of her difference explicitly that later leads to the realization and conscientization of her difference. Radhika Mohanram's Freudian analysis conceptualizing the child's body is revealing: "The body becomes the visual perception of [a cultural/social entity] rather than an experience" (25). Even though Mohanram emphasizes the development of the child and the correlation between his/her "sensation of space/place" and his/her "historical perspective" (25), the community's view of Janie can be regarded similarly. Inversely, Janie is discriminated against on the bases that later serve as the grounds to be elevated in Eatonville: a) the place she lives at, which indicates a higher class position through the association with whites; b) her class position is backed up even among children by her looks, that is, her "spoiling" by a white woman and her complexion. The antagonism against Janie is fueled by the grown female community ("they mama told 'em [. . .]" [9]), which also indicates the inert power mechanism and the power-related structuring within the female community: daughters are socialized into transparent space by their mothers.

Jonah's also provides palpable examples of the presence of transparent female space in childhood. Exactly the same happens to Amy in Georgia as to Janie: for the girls, not only does her family represent class; she also wants to marry John, the most popular boy, who has also light pigmentation. Russel points out that dating in the African American community often shows a psychological drive to find "pale genes" (115), because "embracing Whiteness is a matter of economic, social, or political survival" (55). Both scenes show the socialization of girls into transparent space along these lines so much so that the structure of the female subspace becomes visible in children's games.

Female communal space is mostly present through its absence. The scarcity of female social ties shows explicitly the subtlety of the working of male transparent space, which renders female social space also spatially fragmented. While familial or domestic spaces as well as ritual space are validated in masculine space, they remain limited, either defined by the location of the home or by the incidence of ritual events. Communal space, which can be regarded primarily as social space, appears in collaboration and under the control of men. In *Their Eyes*, in a mock courtship in Eatonville, young men address Bootsie, Teadi, and Big 'oman and later Daisy, objectifying them as pets and denying them voice in the narrative game. Girls gain their public or social identities under the gaze of the male community. In this scene women are played off against each other, which becomes conspicuous, when they engage in Sartrean serial praxis as "The girls and everybody else help laugh" (63). There is no collaboration between women, only functional junctures as when it is reported regarding a village social event: "The women got together the sweets and the men looked after the meats" (42). In another instance, which often characterizes female relationships in Hurston's works, Janie chases another woman, Nunkie, away, who wanted to make advances to Tea Cake (131). The fact that this happens in the Everglades, the liberating haven for men and women alike, is indicative of Hurston's skepticism infiltrating the narrative. Nevertheless, the event signifies female communal space, which, in this way, denounces female relations based on mutuality, but establishes a competitive framework in favor of men, much in contrast to how critics, for example Komar, like to consider female communality: "The interior of the circle formed by women together describes a newly female social space in which communality outstrips competition" (97). As Pheoby admits on welcoming Janie back in

Eatonville: "An envious heart makes a treacherous ear" (5). The sharp evaluation of the female community is backed up beforehand by the narrator: "The women took the faded shirt and muddy overalls [that is, in which Janie returns to Eatonville] and laid them away for remembrance. It was a weapon against her strength [. . .]" (2).

Nurturing female relationships are formed only between mothers and daughters and the possibility of extrafamilial female relationships is projected by the friendship between Janie and Pheoby. Mother-daughter relations come into foreground in *Jonah's*, when Lucy in her deathbed shares her wisdom with her daughter, Isis, and gives her instructions about what Isis is supposed to do when Lucy is dying. Lucy gives Isis her bed, which is her only property, an act that enhances a direct matrilineal linkage in the book. Similarly to Nanny in *Their Eyes*, Lucy admonishes her daughter by sharing her motherwit with her, further contextualizing Lucy in (gendered) femininity. By giving provisions to Isis, Lucy establishes a communal space as she renders trust and mutuality in the pool of their relationship. She becomes dependent on Isis for voice.

Much as motherwit can be imbued with male coercive practice (as in Nanny's case in *Their Eyes* or Emmeline's in *Jonah's*, whose spatial habit is greatly conditioned by the naturalizing maneuvers of transparent space), it aids the sprouting of nurturing female relationships. In *Jonah's* such a realization of female ties is practically absent for Lucy's hermeneutic isolation from other females. However, in *Their Eyes* Hurston establishes a strong bond between Janie and Pheoby that sets them apart both from male and female transparent spaces. The intimacy of their friendship is realized in that the transmission of the text, that is, of Janie's life story, creates a female genealogy and the backyard a "place of anchoring" (Casey 196).

Apart from these two scarce examples, the shallowness of female communal space of Hurston's Southern black communities is further accentuated by the fact that, in the first place, in *Their Eyes* the black female individual finds support under the protective wings of whites. White paternalism can be seen as power mechanism keeping African Americans in an inferior position—an aspect to be detected in Tea Cake's consciousness: after the hurricane in Palm Beach he states, "So Ah means tuh go where de white folks know me. Ah feel lak uh motherless chile round heah" (164). Tea Cake reciting a traditional African American spiritual—a genre with a culturally centripetal function—may appear absurd in this context, since the spiritual overtly addresses a slave child's yearning for his/her lost parents, and connecting parenthood to whites by a black man is an expression of loss of agency. Regarding communal space, Hurston exercises a powerful critique when she shapes a protective white female circle around Janie. Not only can it be seen as a tribute to Hurston's white female Maecenas, but also as a harsh criticism of the black community, which, in Hurston's judgment and despite her devotedness to it, devises also a strong parochial and provincial aspect. In *Their Eyes* Janie experiences the protection of white females twice. First, at the beginning of Janie's quest Mrs. Washburn's care and the antagonism of black girls and women are contrasted: "Mis' Washburn helped out uh whole heap wid things" (10), while black girls instigated by their mothers mock Janie. Then, at the end of the work, Janie finds refuge from her own in the understanding embrace of white women in the court room. There it is spatially neatly depicted that "The white women made a little applause [. . .]" (178) and "[they] cried and stood around her like a protecting wall [. . .]" (179), while the black mass appears marginalized as a depersonalized wall of animosity. In this sense, the courthouse becomes a metaphor of moral space, in which justice is administered in a mothering environment and recognition is granted, which is why Janie goes "to visit the kind white friends who had realized her feelings and thank them" (179). The two scenes show that Janie ends up where she sets out from regarding spatial paradigms.

Hurston's conceptualization of transparent, oppressive space represents masculine domination "by defining a particular intersection between a spatial order and a system of surveillance" (Wigley 332) through the positioning of the female body in space and time, as well as through praxis, that is, ritual and work—both empowering for men and assigning gender roles to women. For Hurston's women, regardless of their class status, the limiting, enclosed context materializes via private, domestic places, the familial context, in which transparent space is realized through the domineering presence of the masculine body and through masculine spatial ordering inclusive of the female body; and via public places, where female identity is constituted as the result of the concerted action (verbal and ritual) of the masculine as well as of female community in social space. The African American female community in Hurston's novels can be seen as a dispositif of masculine transparent space; that is, within the latter, it functions as the primary carrier for the socialization into gender for Hurston's female characters. Thus "the pathology of the communal expectations" (Quashie 53) is also detectable in this subspace and renders women "superwoman, matriarch, mule of the world" (53)—all roles assigned to them in masculine transparent space and controlled by the male gaze.

7. Female Places in Masculine Spaces: Hurston's Feminine Spatiality

Even though Hurston acknowledges masculine transparent social space that denotes the superimposed position of the masculine, she moves beyond the simple binary of masculine and feminine and establishes female subjectivity and feminine sense of place apart from (or notwithstanding) masculine social space, yet within it. Hurston envisions places constructed by women—that is, place constituting identity, not producing it—and a space in which women negotiate identities for themselves through subjective praxis. These places represent thirding in Soja's and Bhabha's sense and function as individual centers of meaning enframed by the masculine social space; that is, apart from it, opposing it, yet depending on it for identity.

As a result, we can count on the presence, even if only through its lack, of the masculine in Hurston's feminine spaces as well, which produces not only opposition, but also cohesive interrelation. So even though Hurston's strategy is to envision feminine private places constructed by women, in which women negotiate identities for themselves through, for instance, ritual praxis, Hurston's feminine "spaces-off" are ambivalent in nature. De Lauretis's term also entails such an interpretation: space-off means ultimately place elsewhere, not in the centre, but constructed in opposition to the hegemonic spatial discourse. Space-off suggests relationality; furthermore, it also devises spatial tactics that are characteristic of the masculine hegemonic discourse. For instance, female social space renders male presence limited as it becomes conspicuous when Lucy dies in *Jonah's*. In this scene John is excluded from the death ritual and is clearly marginalized. Thus De Lauretis's claim of "movement in and out of gender" (26) cannot mean the abolition of gender in the space-off, as masculine transparent space and feminine spaces "coexist concurrently and in contradiction" (26), and gender has as much sense in the latter as in the former. Rather, we witness the inversion of gender in these other spaces juxtaposed to (even if within) transparent space. Only in this (pluralizing) way can De Lauretis's assertion of "multiplicity" and "heteronomy" be regarded as applicable.

In addition, the concept of space-off suggests that feminine spaces and places, and thus feminine subjectivity, are not merely socio-ideological constructs. And this is true for Hurston's fiction too. Even if not indicated directly in the text, her female characters perform their subjectivities, as well as they enact them in their bodies, and inscribe and reinscribe space socially and individually, proving an always already presence of the subject as a "holistic, irreducible unit" (Eshelman, "Postmodernism" 1) despite a panoptic context. In fact, the subject cannot *not* be and, therefore, it is able to resist contextualization, that is, totalization. As Raoul Eshelman points out, elaborating on the novel move of generative anthropology that he calls "performatism": "Subjectivity and semiosis are no longer treated as context-dependent, continually failing gestures but rather form closed, performatively realized wholes that resist dispersal in surrounding contexts" ("Postmodernism" 2). Hurston's feminine subjects go through a process from a position with gendered identities through a "vertiginous progression toward deconstruction of identity" and "molecularization of the self" (Eshelman, "Architecture" 16) to nomadism. This process differs from Bradiotti's proposition in that for Hurston's women "territories are not be crossed in the nomad's never-ending journey" (17) in order to secure boundary transgression for its own sake, but through a journey to (re)connect to place and self, to the "originary ostensive" in Eric Gans's term. In this way, nomadism marks for Hurston's women ability to transgress and use space; and the resistance of contextualization means for her female characters that they are able to both connect to masculine social space (which, at the most, can mean partial contextualization) and establish their own places through "the ability to manipulate time, space, and causality for their own benefit" (Eshelman, "Postmodernism" 4). For Hurston, stability of the minimal self[31] through connectedness to place is an imperative, and the creative, existential use of space a must.

Accordingly, Hurston's female places evolve in private or public masculine places in the first place, as they are tightly connected to the positioning of the female body. There are three kinds of female places detectable in the works under discussion, which also function as signifiers of these women's stage of development of these women and the degree of maturation of their subjectivity: domestic space, the (back) yard, and places outside the former, for example, outside built environment. These are physical, geographic locales, where, apart from their bodies as minimal places, Hurston's women can identify with the environment freely.

Even if the particular female character lives on her own as Nanny in *Their Eyes* does, her place is situated in and surrounded by transparent space. The constraint of race complements the first stage of Janie's life as she and Nanny lived "in de white folks' back yard" (9). Her sense of place is determined to an extent by Washburn's place so that, as Janie reports, "Ah didn't know Ah wuzn't white till Ah was round six years old" (8). Her reduced self is also shown by the fact that at the Washburns's she does not even have a name; she is called "Alphabet" for her many names. Furthermore, stigmatized by the place, she is excluded from the ring plays by the other, black children (8).

---

[31] Hurston's idea of a minimal self is in contrast to Christopher Lasch's concept, who, in a Freudean manner, conceptualizes the minimal self as an ambivalent entity in the function of a "tension between the desire for union and the fact of separation" (177). For Hurston it signifies stability supported by spatial embeddedness.

Janie's genuine sense of place, which characterizes her feminine place-construction, is revealed at Nanny's place, and it is closely connected to a "blossoming pear tree in the back yard" (10). This all-important scene marks her sexual awakening, the advent of her maturing subjectivity, as well as her socialization into gender. The ambivalence of Hurston's space can be pinpointed in the body politics that the tree also expresses: on the one hand, subjugating power mechanism in a patriarchal world through the fecundating activity of active bees and, on the other, traditionally, female wisdom and history, as well as the engendering of an autonomous horizon of expectations. Home for Janie, in Yi-Fu Tuan's terms, becomes the place demarcated by the pear tree. It is a place of knowledge and domination through meaningful epistemology. More concretely, the tree-signified territory is displayed in this scene as a depositor of "deeply meaningful memories and experiences" (Rose 47). In line with Gillian Rose's argument concerning feminization of place, one can easily admit that, via the tree trope, "place is represented as Woman" (56) enframed by masculine social space. For Hurston the back yard and nature in general become private and, more significantly, feminine representations as it is also implied, for instance, by Robert Hemenway.[32]

The duality of resistance, even if through apparently passive subjectivity, and masculine domination becomes conspicuous when Janie cries out, "Oh to be a pear tree—any tree in bloom!" (16). She redoubles the idea of passivity through Freudian imagery and acknowledges male domination represented by the independent bee; however, Janie's revelation under the pear tree endows her with a source to subjectivity, which is why she keeps coming back to it, to think and meditate there (27). It grants her a filter, a set of expectations, and a value hierarchy independent from the male world, although interconnected with it. Female wisdom and history further materialize through an analogy with Nanny's tree-like body, proving also a specific feminine subjectivity through the tree symbolism—much as Nanny can be regarded as an agent of masculine transparent space. Janie cools Nanny's head with herbs, which "looked like the standing roots of some old tree that had been torn away by storm" (17), which by connecting womanhood to nature reconnects Janie's subjectivity to that of Nanny's, that is, to a feminine genealogy.

The scene with the pear tree shows explicitly how a particular place can be symptomatic of space: the autonomy of the self does not denote a hermeneutically sealed development of subjectivity. Hurston proves that power precedes knowledge (even if, at the same time, it does not obliterate it) and, thus, it conditions meaning. Brian Stock reveals that "a significant text is

---

[32] Describing Arvay's psychic world in Hurston's *Seraph on the Suwanee*, Hemenway identifies her self as closely associated with nature, that is, with "the 'great swamp' near [their] home, a dark and murky wilderness that symbolizes the fearful tangle of Arvay's subconscious" (309).

embedded in the place; and it can be recognized by the viewer as falling in the class of literary tropes that he already knows" (315), which for him suggests "pre-read texts" (320). In this way, coercive and contesting as Janie's sense of place may appear, the pollinating bee entails active power despite the apparently overruling proportion of the tree representing Janie. The example of the pear tree reveals that, as Foucault argues, power functions in subtle ways ("Questions on Geography" 72). Resistance and the focus on freedom as sense of place incorporate also preread power mechanisms that influence territorialization and result in ambivalence.

The visionary pear tree in bloom engenders for Janie a specific and subjective sense of place, and its consequent lack conditions her behavior powerfully:

> She was sixteen. She had glossy leaves and bursting buds and she wanted to struggle with life but it seemed to elude her. Nothing on the place nor in her grandma's house answered her. She searched as much of the world as she could from the top of the front steps and then went on down to the front gate and leaned over to gaze up and down the road. Looking, waiting, breathing short with impatience. Waiting for the world to be made. (11)

The vivid description shows Janie's maturation and, spatially, her effort to make use of Nanny's house, that is, to enliven it, as well as Janie's final disenchantment with Nanny's house. Hurston's description is existentially even more relevant as her alienation is heightened by Nanny's penetrating antagonism: "Her [Nanny's] eyes didn't bore and pierce. They diffused and melted Janie, the room and the world into one comprehension" (12). The palpable coinage demonstrates the extreme mechanism of power, as elaborated on previously, as not only is Janie's body marginalized and positioned unwillingly in space, but the contours of her body, those of the minimal self, are attacked. Her newly emerging sense of place denoting her subjectivity symbolized by the blossoming pear tree is endangered.

The other striking aspect of Janie attempting to enliven Nanny's place is how her habitus urges her to construct her own place, but it also characterizes the nature of her sense of place, which is tied to an immaterial, visionary place. Bourdieu conceptualizes habitus as a "strategy-generating principle" (*Outline* 72) and as "universalizing mediation" (79), which "reproduce[s] regularities [as] history turned into nature" (78). Thus habitus is rooted in past experiences and reoccurs as a horizon of expectations in present situations. Searching the world from the top of the steps means searching out the horizon, but not so much the geographic environment as the regions of her mind. Such confabulation— "wherein the remembering subject intercalates fictitious elements or events into memory without awareness of the intercalation" (Casey, "Stompin'" 230)—is activated by her habitus. It is enabled by "the demands of the current situation and past activity" (Schatzki 698), and, through the mediation of confabulation, "habitus generates action" (698). Janie's daydreaming engendering, what Foucault calls, "countermemory" (Braidotti 25) is an ultimate characteristic of Hurston's women.

The tree metaphor plays a significant role at Killicks's place, accompanying Janie all her life. Similarly to Lucy in *Jonah's*, Janie is urged to identify with the gender roles by "Nanny and the old folks" (20) and tries to render Killicks's house motivated for herself. In this way, the collective attempt at socializing her into gender seems successful as she accepts initially the gender divides spatially within the home, as well as she even inscribes gendered space, when she insists on her own domestic territories such as the kitchen (30). This notion proves her need of place-construction and sense of place, and also the crack in hegemonic spatial tactics that enables Janie to use even gendered space creatively and for her own goals.

Besides domestic places, the yard takes a central position in the spatial discourse. Moving to the yard to work under a "fine oak tree" (26) is her first attempt to break away from gendered environment. There she is able to enact her vision of the pear tree authentically. The recuperation to the vision prompted by the trope of the tree pinpoints Janie's nomadic character as this scene marks, for the first time, nomadic cohesion in Bradiotti sense: it is "engendered by repetitions, cyclical moves, [and] rhythmical displacement" (22). The oak tree can be identified as the first cyclical move in Janie's journey. Not only does the firm stature of the oak tree releasing associations with an ancient setting suggest so, but, and especially in contrast to the desolate atmosphere of Killicks's house, the sensuous description of the moment reminiscent of her vision. It is springtime—the time of blossoms—and "the noon filtered through the leaves of the fine oak tree where she sat and made lacy patterns on the ground" (26). In this condensed scene the lacy patterns reveal really what goes on in her. If the scene is compared to how Lucy prepares and decorates her wedding bed with "homemade lace" (81), a common pattern emerges. She is waiting for the visionary to happen as she does previously under the pear tree, when she hears whistling and her future husband appears.

Jonah's presents the relevant female characters, Amy and Lucy, captives of domestic places. In Amy's case nature enforces limitation even more. It does not present her boundless with opportunities and the possibility of freedom in Alabama, as Amy lives on the wrong side of "de Big Creek" (14) among sharecroppers. Here social and economic opportunities are strongly curtailed by the geographic location and limitedness of nature—its barrenness signifying her own. Her forlornness explains why she felt free only "for a minute" and had to return to the house, where she could experience relative autonomy in gendered space—a seeming contradiction.

It is indeed in the domestic sphere for both Amy and Lucy, where they can establish their own places, even if those powerfully intermingle with masculine transparency, and can only obtain a degree of *"transcendent functionalism"* (Eshelman, "Architecture" 4) characteristic of subjective places. Feminine places in *Jonah's* owe their nature to the juxtaposition of the two spaces, while the culturally dominant masculine is superimposed over the feminine. The two coexist, nevertheless, and feminine private places do retain a definite degree of subjectivity. Amy is, for instance, able to construct her own place in the home with the help of her children by relying on "spatially mediated, minimal relations" (Eshelman, "Architecture" 4) that form a distinctive family space in opposition to her husband Ned.

Lucy, similarly to Janie, can initially discover only an immaterial world for herself at her parents' place because her class-conscious mother, ideologizing gender relations, seeks to exert total control over her. Emmeline represents the same African American middle-class code Joe Starks does in Eatonville. By insisting on "proper" gender relations and by policing Lucy closely when John courts her, Emmeline seeks to instill gender consciousness of her class into Lucy, but without success. Even though, unlike Janie's explicitly illuminated vision of the pear tree, Lucy experiences the same revelation—and thus new horizons and a sense of place—in a moment John squeezes her arm and "in a flash she discovered for herself old truths" (68). These prelapsarian truths are, of course, contrary to Emmeline's gender code of masculine space, and their realization by Lucy indicates the advent of a definite subjectivity for her. As it is reported of her the next morning after the encounter with John: "Lucy found a hair upon her body and exulted" (68). This echoes Janie's resolution after her vision of the pear tree: "So this was a marriage!" (11). Lucy's response is identical: "Ahm a woman now" (68). Her revelation may seem childish at first, but it becomes especially significant in a closely policed environment. Not only does this scene signify sexual awakening for Lucy and her declaration an act of subjectivity, this "step away from childhood" (69) also loosens her ties to her mother and detaches Lucy from the parental place. In the selfconscious reassertion of her emerging womanhood, opposition to the gender conceptions of the black middle-class mimicking of white middle-class ideological notions concerning gender is shaping up. By voicing who she is, Lucy designates a place of her own, in this case her body as minimal place, juxtaposing her world and the *other* in a pluralist, or rather, coercive fashion—as Janie does in *Their Eyes* several times.

"Unsilencing" (DuPlessis 108) becomes conspicuous when Lucy talks back to her mother on the day of her wedding, evoking the feminine tree metaphor employed in Hurston's works: "Ahm telling anybody, ole uh young, grizzly or gray, Ah ain't takin' no whipping tuhnight. All mah switches done growed to trees" (78). bell hooks paraphrases struggle in her *Talking Back* powerfully:

> Moving from silence into speech is for the oppressed, the colonized, the exploited, and those who stand and struggle side by side a gesture of defiance that heals, that makes new life and growth possible. It is that act of speech of "talking back," that is no mere gesture of empty words, that is the expression of our movement from object to subject—the liberated voice. (9)

It must be noted, however, that unsilencing is not merely a language-specific action as hooks suggests (28), but a performative action in the line of De Lauretis's movement to space-off, whereby the pantheon of cultural performance is applied. Indeed, if the struggle of Hurston and her female characters is "the search for self and community" (Awkward 5), unsilencing is a cultural act of reimmersion.

In her marriage Lucy's place-construction remains ambiguous. Her life is extremely limited spatially, and she is defenseless against her husband's promiscuous and sometimes brutal behavior; she cannot evade socialization into gender despite her promising vision beforehand. Similarly, however, to characters in performatist fiction, who often "find themselves encased in a frame or rigid set of circumstances that they transcend by reverting to reduced states of consciousness and/or by focusing on simple, opaque things" (Eshelman, "Architecture" 1), Lucy manages to redeem her inner self too. Thus she has to make do with what she has: her feminine private place derives from the identification with the walnut bed, the symbol of marriage. The bed shapes the outer contours of her extended self and so "She made it a spread and bolster of homemade lace" (81). Especially in opposition to the following paragraph that describes John's permissive concept of marriage in violent contrast to Lucy's, this sentence shows not only her attention to detail and the effort she puts into shaping her home, but also her hopes penetrating her sense of place that she realizes spatially. The bed also represents "paradoxical space" (150)—to use Gillian Rose's term—because of its overlapping functions that "complement and contest each other" (160): it both fulfills a regulatory role for Lucy as it appears as the prime vehicle of conditioning her life and grants her space where she can enjoy relative autonomy for a while in Alabama. No wonder that Hurston uses it as the main trope to illuminate Lucy's utmost deprivation: when she is pregnant and conscious of John's unfaithfulness, Bud, her brother, comes to collect her debt in her poverty, and it is the bed he takes away. Only the feather mattress remains, a vague and tormented reminder of her most intimate autonomy: "Lucy was shivering and weeping upon the feather mattress" (91).

Even though Eatonville does not change Lucy's basic position as she remains characteristically in domestic sphere, where she cannot construct a place for herself solely on her own for John's regulating presence wedging into it, Lucy's role changes dramatically. Spatially it is shown by the bed itself, which this time she earns by sewing for a white woman (130). However, she defines herself clearly with respect to and in the function of her husband already before Eatonville: "Ah wants mah husband tuh be uh great big man [. . .]. Ah wants tuh uphold yuh in eve'ything" (96). But in Eatonville she takes a more active role in determining family matters; moreover, she decides about her husband's career plans. As an *éminence grise*, she conditions her husband (despite his will: "Dat's uh bigger job Ah wants tuh tackle, Lucy. You so big-eyed" [109]) to buy a five-acre land and to take on better jobs; e.g., carpentering and later preaching, and, as he growingly accepts Lucy's work ethic and "maneuvering" (116), he even becomes the mayor in Eatonville as well as moderator in the state. Her will-to-power is also well perceived by the Eatonville community: in a porch talk, for instance, Walter Thomas exclaims: "Aw, 'tain't you, Pearson, [. . .] iss dat li'l' handful uh woman you got on de place" (109); and Sam Mosely adds: "Anybody could put hisself on de ladder wid her in de house" (110); and later on he is called "Uh wife-made man" (113). Lucy's prestige and her leading role from the background become even more palpable in the aftermath of the campaign for mayorship when Lucy's role in winning the campaign is repeatedly emphasized.

Lucy's acceptance by the community, unlike Janie's in Eatonville after her rebirth, derives from both Lucy's acceptance of the possible horizon granted to her by masculine space and the consequent construction of "personal networks" (however, not necessarily with other women) that prove both "enabling and constraining" (Gilbert 616). Even if it is her to push and shove John ahead (116), she never exceeds the space ascribed to her, that is, domestic space with the role of a mother, and social space with satellite roles beside her husband, tied to his identity. Lucy's female places remain thus limited despite the upward movement she makes socially and her firmer and widened anchorage existentially. Her confinement is rendered conspicuous many times in the work, but, perhaps, most vividly by the high degree of her immobility. When Lucy and John converse, it happens in their home, where John receives instructions, but, when Lucy is in need, she is left alone in the home and her habitus does not allow her to flee to another place, e.g., nature as John or Janie does in *Their Eyes*. As she cannot hope for help in the physical, social world, her world can only develop inwardly, but there "only the coldness grew numerous" (115). In fact, the only time she oversteps her boundaries is when, sick as she is, she talks back to John: "Ah ain't going' tuh hush nothin' uh de kind. [. . .] Me and mah chillun got some rights" (128). Her reassertion of the self shows her selfawareness and also the power she gains from family space, as well as her position in transparent social space, but she clearly overrates it—also indicated spatially initially as John is towering over her and she is lying in the bed below him: she is stopped abruptly by John hitting her. John's act shatters her world so much so that Lucy begins preparing to die, which is indicated by her giving her only property, the bed, to Isis. She never leaves the bed again; the room remains frozen in that scene, the countdown is implied by the descending movement by a spider on the ceiling.

Besides the tree metaphor, the trope of the road signifies for Hurston the possibility of selffulfillment. As already mentioned, the nonplace-like roads possess a dual function for Hurtson's women, representing also the horizon for them. Several times Janie contemplates the road—e.g., at Nanny's and then at Killicks's place. But even beyond engendering expectations for her, they symbolize a space-off for her outside built environment. Female private places (that is, back yards and natural environments) share a common aspect, which is the detachedness from transparent built environment.

Furthermore, the open space of the roads also symbolizes a qualitative difference in these women's strategy of (also culturally bound) opposition. Namely, by escaping to roads, while moving away from built environment, the female subject a) sets up a nature-culture binary (culture meaning masculine social space); and b) abandons the social in favor of the individual. In fact, as Janie's movement becomes analogous to the dancing body, "presentic movement [of which] interrupts the historical time-frame and creates a space of 'wide-openness'—an unlimited and undetermined time-space of unforeseen possibilities" (Clark-Rapley 104). Roads are liminal places and embody a space of action, where Hurston's female subject is free to establish herself.

It must be acknowledged, however, that Janie's habitus based on her vision conditions Janie's sense of place at these open places. Both times she sets out on roads she does for men, Starks and Tea Cake; that is, Hurston determines the subjectivity of her female characters closely in relation to men. Nevertheless, Janie's liberation is explicit when she breaks away from Killicks:

The morning road air was like a new dress. That made her feel the apron tied around her waist. She untied it and flung it on a bush beside the road and walked on, picking flowers and making a bouquet. [. . .] From now on until death she was going to have flower dust and springtime sprinkled over everything. A bee for her bloom. Her old thoughts were going to come handy now, but new worlds would have to be made and said to fit them. (31)

The wonderful contrast between the refreshing dawn and the apron, a symbol of masculine socialization of women into domestic space, makes palpable Janie's new consciousness, as she obtains temporarily "masculinist hypermobilty" (Pratt and Yeoh 160). Also the high degree of her sense of liberation thrusts forth in the act of getting rid of the apron and collecting flowers in a free and childlike manner. Her spontaneous behavior and "nondirected and nonlimited movement" (qtd. in Clark-Rapley 104) can be compared to the naturalness of improvisational dance, in which, as Elaine Clark-Rapley evaluates it, the "dancing body moves within space, inhabits space," whereby "the body is the apex or point of reference" (103). Her sense of place inhabits space for a short time through her reaching back and recuperating her vision. The "nostalgia for fixity" (Bradiotti 22) apparently counters Bradiotti's concept of the nomad; however, it is this vision that urges Janie to undertake the quest for self in a "[mode] of definite, seasonal patterns of movement through rather fixed routes" (22) that yet reasserts nomadism in this context too. Fixed routes bear special importance also in this scene from the point of view of Hurston's geopolitics. When it is narrated that "Janie hurried out of the front gate and turned south" (31), not only is the direction of Janie's pilgrimage indicated, but also, by way of contrast, the region where African Americans can attain what Janie experiences in the following moments.

Especially in the context of Janie's cyclical patterns of movement also paralleling blues methodology (see Maria V. Johnson), roads for Hurston become thus indeed a metaphor of a particular nomadism in the search of self and place embedded in a region of cultural space. The transformation of roads renders this connection palpable: they carry Janie south and disembogue into a landscape, where there is "Wild cane on either side of the road hiding the rest of the world [and] People [are] wild too" (123). Whereas roads north from the Everglades are framed by houses, modernism, and, in general, masculine transparent space, here the boundaries between nature and culture are deconstructed, as Ann R. Morris and Margaret M. Dunn point out about contemporary Florida, "[t]he migrant workers on the muck govern their lives by the crops; the Seminoles in the glades watch the earth for signs" (5). The symbiosis is also depicted by the roads as they become akin in their nature to the surrounding landscape: "Dirt roads so rich and black that a half mile of it would have fertilized a Kansas wheat field" (123).

For Janie Eatonville grants similar aspects of social upward mobility to Lucy's. She becomes the "bell cow" for the community, but it means ultimately incarceration into overmythicized middle-class femininity with all its ambiguities in an African American community in the Deep South, and physical and social limitation. In the first place, however, her status as a satellite of Starks's marks the confutation of her subjectivity envisioned in the tree trope. Starks's "homo economicus" nature disenchants Janie's resurfacing dreamwork revealed in the ecstatic moments under the oak tree in Killicks's yard and on the road just before. Shortly after their arrival in Eatonville her spatial practice in a manner of De Ceratau's walking-like reinscription of space is shattered as "the new lumber was rattling off the wagon and being piled under the big live oak tree" (38). It is surely not by chance that the timber is hauled exactly under a tree characterized in this way. The "life oak tree" stands for Janie and her sense of place as a direct continuation of both visions under trees previously; the reference to its size embodies the amplitude of her expectations reborn and, at the same time, threatened by desacralizing industrialization. Moreover, the rattling sound contrasts sharply both the alto chant of bees and the homely atmosphere under the tree in Killicks's yard.

The threat of annihilating the tree engendering Janie's subjectivity is overridden when "Jodie moved his things and moved downstairs" (77). After this Janie is beginning to really reinscribe space (also via body politics right after his death as she reclaims her body with her "exhibitive and performative" hairstyle [Newman Phillips 38]). After Janie's long-time subversion, spatial inversion shows that Starks's is losing power over Janie, while Janie is getting hold of the heart of the house: the private spheres. The meaning of the house changes ultimately with Starks's death, and, as also Gaston Bachelard explains the nature of houses, the house grows to symbolize the self as it is turned into *"felicitous space"* (xxxi). First it can be detected when Janie is afraid to go home alone at night: "it was no place to show her fear there in the darkness between the house and the store" (94). An "architectonic closure" takes place in the narrative as the house comes to signify security; it has become a private place for her, and the embodiment of her extended self, or as Bachelard puts it, the "topography of [her] intimate being" (xxxiii). It becomes the symbol of the pear tree in blossom that is waiting for a bee to sink into the sanctuary of her bloom.

The progress of Tea Cake winning Janie's heart is paralleled clearly with Tea Cake's advancing toward the house and entering it. First he appears in the store; the next time they meet, he accompanies Janie to the house onto the porch, which, by then, signifies the outer layers of her social, public self, or, as Clare Cooper puts it, the "public exterior" (131); the same evening he is allowed closer when they do the washing up together in the kitchen (97-98)—the latter representing in many cultures "both a sacred and functional space" (Mazumdar 163) a transitional space outside the private. The third time he enters the "intimate interior" (Cooper 131) by walking into the living room without asking to play the piano. This time he ends up playing with Janie's hair as if with some strings of a musical instrument (99). It is there he confesses his love for her while Janie is standing at the newel post blocking the way leading up to her bedroom. The fourth time Tea Cake visits Janie "they went inside and their laughter rang out first from the kitchen and all over the house" (103). The fact that their laughter fills the entire house indicates that Janie's vision of the tree and a bee finds physical materialization. The texture of the embodied self becomes the house at that moment. One expects what also happens: the next morning they are in bed, "Tea Cake almost kissing her breath away" (103).

The major breakthrough in Janie's development comes when in the Everglades "her soul crawled out from its hiding place" (122). From the point of view of spatial analysis, this "exterirorization of the mind" (Zimm 67) signifies Janie's metamorphosis completed. This quote shows, how—in Gans's terminology—the elementary originary in Janie grows to make her last dynamic move: to identify with the nonplace-like or, from another angle, liminoid open space. The curve of her final development becomes visible in the difference between the exaltation in her bedroom with Tea Cake and this scene. It is reported that in the bedroom "after a long time of passive happiness, she got up and opened the window and let Tea Cake leap forth to the sky on a wind" (103). Here, despite her sense of happiness and liberation, Janie remains in enclosed space and built environment, which stands in sharp contrast to Florida's Southern open landscapes. She opens the window, a clear spatial indication of the dissolution of her previous inner fortification that was built up in an answer to Starks's harassments ("She stood there until something fell off the shelf inside her. She went inside there to see what it was" [67].). Outgoing in Casey's sense represents the beginning of her subsequent transformation into Braidotti's nomadic subject as Janie is able to "free the activity of thinking from the hold of phallocentric dogmatism, returning thought to its freedom, its liveliness, its beauty" (8), or, from another (African American) angle, the last move in completing her blues performance. Still, similarly to Lucy, for whom this is the most she can reach, Janie does not leave the bedroom (the house of her self) to meet the outside world in order to materialize her vision, uniting body and soul, in the exterior context. At this point she is only able to persist on the level of mental and spiritual endeavors metaphorized by her looking up to the sky, but remaining standing on the earth in a room. The importance of Florida for Janie lies in finding a space-off, where she manages to unite body and soul and to contextualize herself in a cultural space that does not discard her unitary originary subjectivity, but enhances it.

Her space-off is even then intact when Janie reaches the final stage of her development in her marriage with Tea Cake. Todd McGowan argues that Janie can obtain momentary freedom after she kills Tea Cake (5), but regarding even the subtlety of previous frameworks Janie is forced into, her act of killing Tea Cake signifies rather Hurston's suture of her own disappointment with marriage into the novel, and in this way, the momentary shattering of Hurston's "metaphysical optimism" (Eshelman, "Postmodernism" 8). I must agree with Selwyn R. Cudjoe who claims that "a person is not complete until she locates herself fully in her time (history) and her place (geography)" (qtd. in Olga Idriss Davis, par. 7). Janie reaches, via transpatial migration across the Southern landscape, an "amorphous" state of existence "connected to many identities" (Gatson 40), that is, not simply gendered first and foremost, but, unlike Sarah N. Gatson's identification of amorphous individuals, she reconstructs her self by finally "validating self [and] rhetorically reconstructing the past (Olga Idriss Davis, par. 9) in her sovereign private place: her back yard.

While it is the shared experience in gendered space and praxis reinscribing space that connect women in Hurston's fiction too, for Janie these represent also ways to distance herself from masculine space and other women likewise. Her feminine spatiality renders her subjectivity autonomous; however, she hybridizes properties of masculine space and transposes them into the feminine, unlike other women of the Eatonville community. Clear instances of the latter are the games she plays such as checkers and shooting, as well as the man she is associated with—all of them transgress boundaries. In fact, a "deconstructive playfulness" (McGowan 1) characterizes the praxis she devises in her new spatial framework.

As for Tea Cake, I have already indicated men's socialization into gender and the implications of power relations for men in masculine social space. Tea Cake in this framework occupies a subordinate position also spatially expressed, even if his position can be seen as ambivalent: he never settles, so socially he is placeless and marginalized, but his freedom derives exactly from his social exclusion and his consequent physical mobility. In a systematic practice of thirding, Janie, by associating with him, transgresses, but, at the same time, transcends the boundaries of social space, especially its class and gender constrains. On Starks's side Janie acquires previously a middle-class status and later a prestigious position of a well-to-do widow, who is supposed to maintain proper gender relations, while remaining in gendered space. Tea Cake represents the negation of gender ideology by being younger and poorer, and through his praxis and gender conceptions, particularly in contrast to other males courting Janie. By choosing Tea Cake, Janie inverts masculine space by the de-re-construction of gender (De Lauretis 24), which becomes really visible in the figure of Hezekiah, who helps out in the store: Janie, the owner of the store, standing higher in the social hierarchy than the seventeen year old boy also because of her age, develops the habit of playing checkers on the porch, which previously was a tool in Starks's hand in her subordination (one time Starks orders Janie, "Go fetch de checker-board *and* de checkers" [71], meaning that Janie is not intelligent enough to play a male's game), while Hezekiah ("the best imitation of Joe" in his habits, at which "she laughed outright" [87, 88]) remains in the store to work instead of Janie.

By letting Janie reassert her subjectivity through hybridization and through drawing a map of "counter topography" (Pratt and Yeoh 163) in physical space, Hurston distances her character from her community via bordercrossing, and particularly from the race-, gender-, class ideology that penetrates the African American community. Janie inverts both gender and class conventions by transgressing gender boundaries imbued with class ideology, and Hurston exerts a powerful critique of "the race" by ironically separating Janie from mainstream ideals also in space. By allowing Janie to enact her vision, Hurston subverts "controlling images" (Simms 879) of the black female, and proposes an autonomous subjectivity yet embedded in a socio-cultural space.

Autonomous subjectivity can be detected in the fact that Janie is able to form a communal space with her friend. However, Hurston deconstructs female transparent space individually and socially already before the Everglades. Hurston's strategy is not to construct an entirely new, alternative universe, which is ultimately proved by the devastation in the Hurricane scene, but to build in fissures in masculine and female transparent spaces. In the focal point of these schisms one can detect the genuinely individual that is able to shape nurturing social relations as well.

It is Southern black cultural space, where Hurston's female characters reach ultimately the horizon of their female subjectivities and sense of place. It is not that gendered space becomes overridden, but, rather, Hurston constructs a space, in which gender relations are embedded in a pluralist context. On the muck in *Their Eyes* female and masculine spaces are juxtaposed in natural heterotopia and, at the same time, intertwined not to abolish gender, but to form an integrated space (from a womanist perspective) of a large variety of mosaics. Janie's overalls undergird this statement as they symbolize "nice bit of cross-dressing, signifying equality and sexuality in gender terms [. . .]" (DuPlessis 25). Thirding renders possible for Janie, for instance, what previously only men have power to do with women: in an inverted, yet parallel scene with *Jonah's*, Janie "cut him [that is, Tea Cake] short with a blow" (131) in a fit of jealousy; and after they make love, "she had to crow over the fallen Nunkie" (132), just as John in *Jonah's* "held Lucy tightly and thought pityingly of other men" (111). This shows the neatness of the mechanism of integrating feminization, problematizing the supposed homogeneity of social space, and effecting polyvalence. For Hurston feminine space-off cuts across gender lines, class boundaries, and it is realized idealistically in the geographic region of Florida, where spacing off is not a matter of life instinct only, but a possibility of choice.

8. Conclusion

I have set the context of the present research by delineating two seemingly mutually exclusive understandings of space: phenomenological place-construction and the post-Marxist production of space. According to the former, the subjective self is the active agent to establish space and places. It is mainly the habitus (based on past experiences) of the subject that influences the inhabiting of a place by a subject. The embodied subject enlivens and organizes space around him/herself. Conversely, in post-Marxist thought the subject is decentered and embedded in a spatial context in which power discourses condition the establishment of the places by the subject; subjects are positioned in places in the same way. Thus places of a social space prove to be dispositifs facilitating the spatial indoctrination and socialization into identity of the Post-Marxian subject.

I have offered a more accommodating (less confrontational) theoretical framework—though not as a synthesis of the two theoretical paradigms—building on the propositions of both schools. Much as the subject encounters social space as a sociopolitical fixity, s/he manages to find ways of boundary crossing via heterotopous juxtaposition and hybridization. These spatial practices entail not only the construction of places apart from places of social space—that is, elsewhere—but also the reworking of previously indoctrinating places. Relying on the theories of Bhabha and Soja, I have referred to the activity of the subject as *thirding*—a praxis reinscribing and restructuring space. Within the given sociospatial fixity, thirding enables refusal of categorization and grants the subject a means to construct his/her places creatively—a testimony of subjectivity.

Relying on the outline of theories of space and place, I have argued that, in her two most renowned novels *Their Eyes Were Watching God* and *Jonah's Gourd Vine*, Hurston constructs a cultural space that can be best conceptualized in the light of her cultural philosophy, which relies on the anthropologist's knowledge of African American culture and her experience of the American (racial and gender) matrix.

Hurston's strategy builds on her knowledge of African American cultural performances and places. She revitalizes cultural performances such as tactics of insiderness, call-and-response, or tricksterism in order to portray the inherent nature of the African American community, as manifested in the relationship between the individual and community. The apparent ambivalence shows attachment to, and interdependence with, the African American community, as well as distancing from it, which can be taken as an act of subjectivation within it. Hurston's fiction thus fulfills the individual's quest both in opposition and in relation to the community. Individual conduct reinforces the African American cultural core—hence necessarily a centripetal performance—instead of transgressing it, and the centre, anticipating apparently dissenting action, reacts to it in a call-and-response communicational pattern. The inherently intracommunal pattern grants Hurston a multidimensional approach to African American culture since improvisation facilitates pluralism and heteronomy within the cultural framework. In Hurston's cultural/cosmological space the construction of places shows similar characteristics: she hybridizes places by inverting them to express the subjectivity of her characters. The resulting lack of fixity is evidence of cultural immersion and manifestation of underground performance in Baker's sense as well as trickster performance in Gates's.

Her writing strategy displays her cultural self. Blending anthropology and literature, she introduces in her writing a constant movement in and out of the paradigms of literature and anthropology, so much so that her novels can be read at times as ethnography with the narrator as a participant observer. In Hurston's cultural philosophy, her writing becomes the disclosure of an authentic cultural space. Despite critical accusations of inauthenticity, Hurston performs an African American cultural act conceptualized as *masking*—an African American reassertion of culture. Her masking strategy, for which her cultural space has been at times dismissed as static, is clearly a sign of her cultural approach to literature, that is, writing from within; not to conceal, but to disclose a world in which heterogeneity establishes cultural variety and dynamism. In this line of thought, it can be explained why Hurston was such a controversial figure of her age. She resisted categorization in all aspects of her life, including her writing.

The playfulness implied by her cultural understanding precipitates in her place construction. Just as African American cultural performance is to be understood in the matrix of community and self, individual place-making exists also within the context of a socio-cultural space—a transparent space which often proves to be indoctrinating, presenting a normative environment with explicit and implicit power-mechanisms, and influences individual place construction. Place-making, however, emerges as a phenomenological entity, intrinsic in subjectivation. In this binary, the question presents itself how.

In Hurston's case, it can rightly be argued that the two constraints, culture (not primarily race) and gender—which justify the examination of an African American cultural and gendered space in Hurston's novels—provide two overlapping spaces to specify different aspects of the same cultural space. In negotiating a place/identity in these spaces, Hurston proceeds with the help of strategies informed by trickster energies to establish an integrated cultural space and network of places, which are simultaneously both encultured (in the sense they represent an African American cultural space) and engendered.

Hurston's rejection of fixity is foregrounded in the nature of her places, both regarding their positioning and their inner structure. I have employed the terms *third space* (Bhabha) and *thirding* (Soja) to identify Hurston's hybridization of place. The strategy implied by these terms pervades all aspects of her cultural space. She turns gendered places into *space-off* to indicate a position of difference underlining the subjectivity of her female characters, transforms African American places into *nonplace* to show the distanced, yet mainstream position of her individuals in relation to African American culture (more specifically, the Harlem Renaissance); and she uses liminal places in her religio-cultural space to allow her subjects an individual (but culturally conditioned) encounter with the numinous.

Thirding suggests that the place established in this way steps out of a narrowing dialectics designating an opposition between transparent space and individual place construction. It does not denote harsh rejection of a social space, the rejection of its places, nor does it mean a pervasive negation of its values. Much rather, one can talk about constituting difference on another level, whereby props (such as place) and strategies (e.g., power mechanisms) of the respective social space are built upon or incorporated into a different, subjective spatiality. This does not imply a synthesis of spaces, but the reinscription of space within that particular social space.

Hurston's employment of a thirding strategy, however, is not simply the reinscription of a sociocultural space. Her intention is to establish an integrated cultural space that allows the African American individual to become an agent within his/her culture. Places of thirding are always related to African American culture; even if located in the in-between, they remain embedded inherently in the sociocultural space Hurston seemingly criticizes. Thirding, therefore, can be identified as a means of cultural inclusion and the instrument of cultural emergence in Hurston's philosophy.

The notion of cultural emergence is most motivated in her religio-cultural space, in which Hurston's main characters, John in *Jonah's* and Janie in *Their Eyes* go to liminal places, where their subjectivation is aided in the axis mundi, as well as they obtain subjectivity at liminal places that connect them intrinsically to the African American tradition via an initiation rite. These places partake in a black sacred cosmos (see Lincoln and Mamiya) informed by African American cosmology and the ritual movement of the African American subject to liminal places.

Hurston's nonplaces and space-offs prove vital in her cultural space since they serve as aids of subjectivation and become communicational interfaces with a motivated African American cultural context. On the one hand, these places present fissures in hegemonic discourses of African American culture and gender, as they project the possibility of agency and the establishment of alternative spatialities; on the other hand, they serve as individual statements as against the mainstream cultural discourse of the Harlem Renaissance and the gender discourse of transparent social space.

Hurston's cultural space proves dynamic despite apparent rigidity. The interplay of space and place dramatizes interaction between them in a way that ensures justification of places regarding the different aspects of social space. Hurston conceptualizes their relation as interrelation and not as superimposition of space over place. The ultimately African American pattern follows the traditional call-and-response dialogicity, whereby places, supposedly of the margin, are complementary categories that embody necessary tethering of the African American cultural core.

Works Cited

Aitken, Stuart, and Christopher Lukinbeal. "Disassociated Masculinities and Geographies of the Road." *The Road Movie Book*. Ed. Steven Cohan and Ina Rae Hark. London: Routledge, 1997. 349-70. Print.

Althusser, Louis. "Contradiction and Overdetermination." *For Marx*. Trans. Ben Brewster. London: Verso, 1985. 87-129. Print.

Ammons, Elizabeth. "Introduction." *Tricksterism in Turn-of-the-century American Literature: A Multicultural Perspective*. Ed. Elizabeth Ammons and Annette White Parks. Hanover, NH: UP of New England, 1994. vii-xiii. Print.

Aravot, Iris. "Back to Phenomenological Placemaking." *Journal of Urban Design* 7.2 (2002): 201–12. Print.

Archer, Neil. "The Road as the (Non-)Place Of Masculinity: *L'Emploi du temps*." *Studies in French Cinema* 8.2 (2008): 137–48. Print.

Arefi, Mahyar. "*Non-place* and Placelessness as Narratives of Loss: Rethinking the Notion of *Place*." *Journal of Urban Design* 4.2 (June 1999): 179-93. Print.

Augé, Marc. *Non-Places: Introduction to an Anthropology of Supermodernity*. Trans. John Howe. London: Verso, 1995. Print.

Awkward, Michael. *Inspiring Influences*. New York: Columbia UP: 1989. Print.

Bachelard, Gaston. *The Poetics of Space*. Trans. Maria Jolas. Boston: Beacon, 1969. Print.

Bachmann-Medick, Doris. "Einleitung." ["Introduction"]. *Kultur als Text: Die Anthropologische Wende in der Literaturwissenschaft*. [Culture as Text: The Anthropological Turn in Literary Scholarship]. Frankfurt am Main: Fischer, 1996. 7-64. Print.

Bakhtin, Mikhail M. *The Dialogic Imagination: Four Essays by M.M. Bakhtin*. 1975. Ed. Michael Holquist. Trans. Caryl Emerson and Michael Holquist. Austin: U of Texas P, 1981. Print.

Baker, Houston A., Jr. *Blues, Ideology, and Afro-American Literature: A Vernacular Theory*. Chicago: U of Chicago P, 1984. Print.

Bartky, Sandra Lee. "Foucault, Femininity, and the Modernization of Patriarchal Power." *Feminism and Foucault: Reflections on Resistance*. Ed. Irene Diamond and Lee Quinby. Boston: Northeastern UP, 1988. 61-86. Print.

Basso, Keith H. *Wisdom Sits in Places: Landscape and Language among the Western Apache*. Albuquerque: U of New Mexico P, 1996. Print.

Baudrillard, Jean. *Simulacra and Simulation*. Trans. Sheila Faria Glaser. Ann Arbor: U of Michigan P, 1994. Print.

Bhabha, Homi. *The Location of Culture*. London: Routledge, 1994.

Biczó, Gábor, and Kiss Noémi. "Szerkesztői Előszó." ["Editor's Introduction"]. *Antropológia és Irodalom: Egy Új Paradigma Keresése*. [Anthropology and Literature: Looking for a New Paradigm]. Ed. Gábor Biczó and Noémi Kiss. Debrecen: Csokonai, 2003. 9-10. Print.

Bordo, Susan. *Twilight Zones: The Hidden Life of Cultural Images from Plato to O. J.* Berkely: U of Californua P, 1997. Print.

---. *Unbearable Weight: Feminism, Western Culture, and the Body.* Berkeley: U of California P, 1993. Print.

Bourdieu, Pierre. *Férfiuralom.* Trans. Zsuzsa N. Kiss. Budapest: Napvilág, 2000. Print.

---. *Outline of a Theory of Practice.* Cambridge: Cambridge UP, 1977. Print.

Botkin, Benjamin Albert. *A Treasury of Southern Folklore: Stories, Ballads, Traditions, and Folkways of the People of the South.* New York: Crown, 1949. Print.

Boyle, Mark. "Sartre's Circular Dialectic and the Empires of Abstract Space: A History of Space and Place in Ballymun, Dublin." *Annals of the Association of American Geographers* 95.1 (2005): 181–201. Print.

Bradiotti, Rosi. "Introduction: By Way of Nomadism." *Nomadic Subjects: Embodiment and Sexual Difference in Contemporary Feminist Theory.* New York: Columbia UP, 1994. 1-40. Print.

Brown, L. B. "Phenomenology of Religion." *The International Journal for the Psychology of Religion* 1.2 (1991): 101-106. Print.

Browning Christopher S., and Pertti Joenniemi. "Contending Discourses of Marginality: The Case of Kaliningrad." *Geopolitics* 9.3 (2004): 699–730. Print.

Butler, Judith. *Bodies that Matter: On the Discursive Limits of "Sex."* London, Routledge, 1993. Print.

---. "Subjects of Sex/Gender/Desire." Gender Trouble. London: Routledge, 1990. 1-34. Print.

Carby, Hazel V. "The Politics of Fiction, Anthropology, and the Folk." *Zora Neale Hurston: Their Eyes Were Watching God. A Casebook.* Ed. Cheryl A. Wall. Oxford, New York: Oxford UP, 2000. 117-36. Print.

Carr, Brian, and Tova Cooper. "Zora Neale Hurston and Modernism at the Critical Limit." *Modern Fiction Studies* 48.2 (2002): 285-313. Print.

Carr-Hamilton, Jacqueline D. "Motherwit in Southern Religion." *"Ain't Gonna Lay My 'Ligion Down": African American Religion in the South.* Ed. Alonzo Johnson and Paul Jersild. Columbia, SC: U of South Carolina P, 1996. 72-87. Print.

Casey, Edward S. "Between Geography and Philosophy." *Annals of the Association of American Geographers* 91.4 (2001): 683-93. Print.

---. "On Habitus and Place." *Annals of the Association of American Geographers* 91.4 (2001): 716-23. Print.

---. *Remembering: A Phenomenological Study.* Bloomington and Indianapolis: Indiana UP, 1987. Print.

---. "Stompin' on Scott: A Cursory Critique of Mind and Memory." *Research in Phenomenology* 30.1 (2000): 223-39. Print.

Cesareo, Mario. "Anthropology and Literature: of Bedfellows and Illegitimate Offspring." *Between Anthropology and Literature: Interdisciplinary Discourse.* Ed. Rose De Angelis. London: Routledge, 2002. Print.

Champion, Tempii B. *Understanding Storytelling among African American Children: A Journey from Africa to America.* Mahwah, NJ: Lawrence Erlbaum, 2003. Print.

Clark-Rapley, Elaine. "Dancing Bodies: Moving beyond Marxian Views of Human Activity, Relations and Consciousness." *Journal for the Theory of Social Behaviour* 29.2 (1999): 89-108. Print.

Clayton, Ronnie W. *Mother Wit: The Ex-Slave Narratives of the Louisiana Writers' Project.* New York: Lang, 1990. Print.

Cooper, Clare. "The House as a Symbol of the Self." *Designing for Human Behavior: Architecture and the Behavioral Sciences.* Ed. Jon Lang et al. Stroudsburg, PA: Dowden, Hutchinson & Ross, 1974. 130-46. Print.

Critchley, Simon. "Enigma Variations: An Interpretation of Heidegger's *Sein und Zeit.*" *Ratio* 15.2 (2002): 154-75. Print.

Curren, Erik D. "Should Their Eyes Have Been Watching God? Hurston's Use of Religious Experience and Gothic Horror." *African American Review* 29.1 (1995): 17-26. *Questia.* Web. 20 March 2007.

Daniel, Jack L., and Geneva Smitherman. "How I Got Over: Communication Dynamics in the Black Community." *Cultural Communication and Intercultural Contact.* Ed. Donal Carbaugh. Hillsdale, NJ: Erlbaum, 1990. 27-40. Print.

Davis, Olga Idriss. "A Black Woman As Rhetorical Critic: Validating Self and Violating the Space Of Otherness." *Women's Studies in Communication* 21.1 (1998): 77-89. Print.

Davis, Rose Parkman. *Zora Neale Hurston: An Annotated Bibliography and Reference Guide.* Westport, CT: Greenwood P, 1997. *Questia.* Web. 17 Dec. 2007.

De Angelis, Rose. "Introduction." *Between Anthropology and Literature: Interdisciplinary Discourse.* Ed. Rose De Angelis. London: Routledge, 2002. Print.

De Certeau, Michel. *The Practice of Everyday Life.* Berkeley: U of California P, 1984. Print.

De Lauretis, Teresa. "The Technology of Gender." *Technologies of Gender: Essays on Theory, Film, and Fiction.* Houndmills: MacMillan, 1987. 1-30. Print.

Deleuze, Gilles. "What is a Dispositif?" *Michel Foucault Philosopher.* Trans. Timothy J. Armstrong. New York: Harvester, 1992. 159-69. Print.

De Weever, Jacqueline. *Mythmaking and Metaphor in Black Women's Writing.* New York: St. Martin's, 1991. Print.

Dixon, Melvin. *Ride out the Wilderness: Geography and Identity in Afro-American Literature.* Chicago: U of Illinois P, 1987. Print.

Domosh, Mona. "Geography and Gender: Home, Again?" *Progress in Human Geography* 22.2 (1998): 276-82. Print.

Dreyfus, Hubert L. "Heidegger's Critique of the Husserl/Searle Account of Intentionality." *Social Research* 60.1 (1993): 17-38. Print.

DuBois, W.E.B. *The Souls of Black Folk.* New York: Dover, 1994. Print.

Durkheim, Émile. *The Elementary Forms of Religious Life.* Trans. Carol Cosman. New York: Oxford UP, 2001. Print.

DuPlessis, Rachel Blau. "Power, Judgement, and Narrative in a Work of Zora Neale Hurston: Feminist Cultural Studies." *New Essays on Their Eyes Were Watching God.* Ed. Michael Awkward. Cambridge: Cambridge UP, 1990. 95-125. Print.

Eliade, Mircea. *Rites and Symbols of Initiation: The Mysteries of Birth and Rebirth.* New York: Harper, 1958. Print.

Eshelman, Raoul. "Performatism in Architecture. On Framing and the Spatial Realization of Ostensivity." *Anthropoetics* 7.2 (2001/2002): n. pag. Web. 30 June 2005.

---."Performatism, or the End of Postmodernism." *Anthropoetics* 6.2 (2000/2001): n. pag. Web. 30 June 2005.

Favor, J. Martin. *Authentic Blackness: The Folk in the New Negro Renaissance.* Durham, NC: Duke UP, 1999. Print.

Fleurant, Gerdès. *Dancing Spirits: Rhythms and Rituals of Haitian Vodun, the Rada Rite.* Westport: Greenwood, 1996. Print.

Foucault, Michel. "Body/Power" *Power/Knowledge: Selected Interviews and Other Writings 1972-1977.* Ed. Colin Gordon. New York: Pantheon, 1980. Print.

---. *Discipline and Punish: The Birth of the Prison.* New York: Vintage/Random, 1995. Print.

---. "Of Other Spaces." *Diacritics* 16 (1986): 22-27. *Jstor.* Web. 10 July 2005.

---. "Questions on Geography." *Power/Knowledge: Selected Interviews and Other Writings 1972-1977.* Ed. Colin Gordon. New York: Pantheon, 1980. 63-77. Print.

---. "Space, Power and Knowledge." *The Cultural Studies Reader.* Ed. Simon During. London: Routledge, 1993. 161-70. Print.

---. "The Subject and Power." *Beyond Structuralism and Hermeneutics.* Ed. Hubert L. Dreyfus and Paul Rabinow. Chicago: U of Chicago P, 1982. 208-26. Print.

Gans, Eric. "Originary Narrative." *Anthropoetics* 3.2 (1997/1998): n. pag. Web. 30 June 2005.

Gates, Henry Louis, Jr. *The Signifying Monkey: A Theory of African-American Literary Criticism*. New York: Oxford UP, 1988. Print.

Gatrell, Jay D., and Jeff Worsham. "Policy Spaces: Applying Lefebvrian Politics in Neo-institutional Spaces." *Space & Polity* 6.3 (2002): 327–42. Print.

Gatson, Sarah N. "On Being Amorphous: Autoethnography, Genealogy, and a Multiracial Identity." *Qualitative Inquiry* 9.1 (2003): 20-48. Print.

Gayle, Addison Jr. "The Outsider." *Zora Neale Hurston*. Ed. Harold Bloom. New York: Chelsea, 1986. 35-46. Print.

Geertz, Clifford. *The Interpretation of Cultures*. New York: Basic, 1973. Print.

Gilbert, Melissa. "'Race,' Space, and Power: The Survival Strategies of Working Poor Women." *Annals of the Association Of American Geographers* 88.4 (1998): 595-621. Print.

Gloria Anzaldúa. *Borderlands/La Frontera: The New Mestiza*. San Francisco: Aunt Lute, 2007. Print.

Gregory, Derek. *Geographical Imagination*. Cambridge: Blackwell, 1994. Print.

Hadas, Miklós. *A modern férfi születése*. [The Birth of Modern Man]. Budapest: Helikon, 2003. Print.

Haddox, Thomas F. "The Logic of Expenditure in *Their Eyes Were Watching God*." *Mosaic* 34.1 (2001): n. pag. *Questia*. Web. 15 Oct. 2008.

Hall, Stuart. "Encoding, Decoding." *The Cultural Studies Reader*. Ed. Simon During. London: Routledge, 1993. 90-102.

---. "The Work of Representation." *Representation: Cultural Representations and Signifying Practices*. Ed. Stuart Hall. London: Sage, 1997. 13-75. Print.

Hanson, Susan, and Geraldine Pratt. *Gender, Work, and Space*. London: Routledge, 1995. Print.

Harvey, David. *The Condition of Postmodernity: An Enquiry into the Origins of Cultural Change*. Cambridge: Blackwell, 1990. Print.

---. *The New Imperialism*. Oxford: Oxford UP, 2003. Print.

Hecht, Michael L. et al. *African American Communication: Exploring Identity and Culture*. Mahwah, NJ: Erlbaum, 2003. Print.

Heidegger, Martin. *Being and Time*. Trans. Joan Stambaugh. Albany: State U of New York P, 1996.

---. "Building Dwelling, Thinking." *Poetry, Language, Thought*. Trans.: Albert Hofstadter. New York: Harper & Row, 1971. 143-61. Print.

Heintzman, Paul. "The Wilderness Experience and Spirituality: What Recent Research Tells Us." *JOPERD* 74.6 (2003): 27-32. *Questia*. Web. 17 June 2007.

Hemenway, Robert E. *Zora Neale Hurston: A Literary Biography*. Urbana: U of Illinois P, 1980. Print.

Hill, Lynda Marion. *Social Rituals and the Verbal Art of Zora Neale Hurston.* Washington: Howard UP, 1996. Print.

Hoffman-Jeep, Lynda. "Creating Ethnography: Zora Neale Hurston and Lydia Cabrera." *African American Review* 39.3 (2005): 337-53. *Questia.* Web. 25 June 2007.

Hofstede, Geert. *Cultures and Organizations: Software of the Mind.* London: McGraw-Hill, 1991. Print.

hooks, bell. *Talking Back: Thinking Feminist, Thinking Black.* Boston: South End,1989. Print.

Hubbard, Dolan. "'. . . Ah Said Ah'd Save De Text for You': Recontextualizing the Sermon to Tell (Her)story in Zora Neale Hurston's *Their Eyes Were Watching God.*" *African American Review* 27.2 (1993): 167-78. *Questia.* Web. 25 June 2007.

Hughes-Warrington, Marnie. "The 'Ins' and 'Outs' of History: Revision as Non-Place." *History and Theory* 46 (December 2007): 61-76. Print.

Hurston, Zora Neale. "Characteristics of Negro Expression." *The Sanctified Church: The Folklore Writings of Zora Neale Hurston.* Berkeley: Turtle Island, 1981. 49-69. Print.

---. *Dust Tracks on the Road.* London: Virago, 1986. Print.

---. *Every Tongue Got to Confess: Negro Folk-tales from the Gulf States.* New York: Harper Collins, 2001. Print.

---. "How It Feels to Be Colored Me." *Zora Neale Hurston: Folklore, Memoirs, and Other Writings.* Ed. Cheryl A. Wall. New York: The Library of America, 1995. 826-30. Print.

---. *Jonah's Gourd Vine.* New York: Harper, 1990. Print.

---. *Mules and Men.* Bloomington: Indiana UP, 1978. Print.

---. "Negro Mythical Places." Go Gator Muddy the Water: Writings by Zora Neale Hurston from the Federal Writers' Project. Ed. Pamela Bordelon. New York: Norton, 1999. 106-12. Print.

---. "Sweat." *Zora Neale Hurston: Novels and Stories.* Ed. Cheryl A. Wall. New York: The Library of America, 1995. 955-67. Print.

---. *Tell My Horse.* New York: Harper, 1990. Print.

---. *The Sanctified Church: The Folklore Writings of Zora Neale Hurston.* Berkeley: Turtle Island, 1981. Print.

---. *Their Eyes Were Watching God.* New York: Harper, 1990. Print.

---. "To Jean Parker Waterbury." *Zora Neale Hurston: A Life in Letters.* Ed. Carla Kaplan. New York: Doubleday, 2002. 645-6. Print.

---. "To Langston Hughes." *Zora Neale Hurston: A Life in Letters.* Ed. Carla Kaplan. New York: Doubleday, 2002. 124. Print

James, Allison, et al. "Introduction: The Road From Santa Fe." *After Writing Culture: Epistemology and Praxis in Contemporary Anthropology.* Ed.

Allison James, Andrew Dawson, and Jenny Hockey. London: Routledge, 1997. Print.

Jameson, Fredric. *Postmodernism, or the Cultural Logic of Late Capitalism.* Durham: Duke UP, 1991. Print.

Johnson, Barbara. "Metaphor, Metonymy and Voice in *Their Eyes Were Watching God.*" *Zora Neale Hurston. Modern Critical Views: Zora Neale Hurston.* Ed. Harold Bloom. New York: Chelsea, 1986. 157-73. Print.

Johnson, Alonzo. "Pray's House Spirit: The Institutional Structure and Spiritual Core of an African American Folk Tradition." *"Ain't Gonna Lay My 'Ligion Down:" African American Religion in the South.* Ed. Alonzo Johnson and Paul Jersild. Columbia: U of South Carolina P, 1996. 8-39. Print.

Johnson, Maria V. "'The World in a Jug and the Stopper in (Her) Hand': *Their Eyes* As Blues Performance." *African American Review* (1998): n. pag. Bnet. Web. 19 Sept. 2004.

Joseph, Philip. "The Verdict from the Porch: Zora Neale Hurston and Reparative Justice." *American Literature* 74.3 (2002): 455-83. Print.

Kaelin, Eugene Francis. *Heidegger's Being and Time: A Reading for Readers.* Tallahassee: UP of Florida, 1988. Print.

Kedia, Satish, and John Van Willigen. "Applied Anthropology: Context for Domains of Application." *Applied Anthropology: Domains of Application.* Ed. Satish Kedia and John Van Willigen. Westport, CT: Praeger, 2005. 1-33. *Questia.* Web. 25 July 2008.

Keller, Catherine. *The Face of the Deep: A Theology of Becoming.* London: Routledge, 2002. Print.

Kelly, Sean Dorrance. "Merlaeu-Ponty on the Body." *Ratio* 15.4 (2002): 376-91. Print.

Keményfi, Róbert. *Földrajzi Szemlélet a Néprajztudományban.* [Geographical Approach in Ethnography]. Debrecen: Kossuth Egyetemi Kiadó, 2004. Print.

Kirby, Steve. "Dimensions and Meanings of Anxiety." *Existential Analysis* 15.1 (2004): 73-86. Print.

Komar, Kathleen. "Feminist Curves in Contemporary Literary Space." *Reconfigured Spheres: Feminist Explorations of Literary Space.* Ed. Margaret R. Higonnet and Joan Templeton. Amherst, MA.: U of Massachusetts P, 1994. 89-108. *Questia.* Web. 28 Nov. 2007.

Kunstler, James Howard. *The Geography of Nowhere: The Rise and Decline of America's Man-Made Landscape.* New York: Touchstone, 1993. Print.

Lasch, Christopher. *The Minimal Self: Psychic Survival in Troubled Times.* New York: Norton, 1984. Print.

Law, Robin. "Beyond 'Women and Transport': Towards New Geographies of Gender and Daily Mobility." *Progress in Human Geography* 23.4 (1999): 567-88. Print.

Lefebvre, Henri. *The Production of Space*. Trans. Donald Nicholson-Smith. Oxford: Blackwell, 1991. Print.

Lemke, Sieglinde. *Primitivist Modernism: Black Culture and the Origins of Transatlantic Modernism*. Oxford, New York: Oxford UP, 1998. Questia. Web. 29 July 2007.

Levinas, Emmanuel. *Totality and Infinity*. Pittsburgh: Duquesne UP, 2001. Print.

Levine, Lawrence W. *Black Culture and Black Consciousness: Afro-American Folk Thought from Slavery to Freedom*. Oxford: Oxford UP, 1978. *Questia*. Web. 25 July 2008.

Lincoln, C. Eric, and Lawrence H. Mamiya. *The Black Church in the African American Experience*. Durham, Duke UP, 1990. Print.

Locke, Alain. "The New Negro." *The New Negro*. Ed. Alain Locke. New York: Atheneum, 1968. 3-16. Web. 25 July 2008.

Logan, Onnie Lee. *Motherwit*. New York: E. P. Dutton, 1989. Print.

Löfgren, Orvar. "The Sweetness of Home: Class, Culture and Family Life in Sweden." *The Anthropology of Space and Place: Locating Culture*. Ed. Setha M. Low and Denise Lawrence-Zúñiga. Malden: Blackwell, 2003. 142-60. Print.

Marcoulatos, Iordanis. "Merleau-Ponty and Bourdieu on *Embodied Significance*." *Journal for the Theory of Social Behaviour* 31.1 (2001): 1-27. Print.

Mazumdar Shampa, and Sanjoy Mazumdar. "'Women's significant Spaces': Religion, Space, and Community." *Journal of Environmental Psychology* 19 (1999): 159-70. Print.

McCann, Eugene J. "Race, Protest, and Public Space: Contextualizing Lefebvre in the U.S. City." *Antipode* 31.2 (1999): 163–84. Print.

McDonogh, Gary W. "Introduction." *The Florida Negro: A Federal Writers' Project Legacy*. Ed. Gary W. McDonogh. Jackson, MS: UP of Mississippi, 1993. vii-xxxv. Print.

McGowan, Todd. "Liberation and Domination: *Their Eyes Were Watching God* and the Evolution of Capitalism." *MELUS* (Spring 1999): n. pag. Bnet. Web. 11 Apr. 2006.

McPherson, James Alan. *Railroad: Trains and Train People in American Culture*. New York: Random, 1976. Print.

Merelman, Richard M. *Representing Black Culture: Racial Conflict and Cultural Politics in the United States*. London: Routledge, 1995. Print.

Merleau-Ponty, Maurice. *Phenomenology of Perception*. Trans. Colin Smith. London: Routledge, 1962. Print.

---. *The Visible and Invisible*. Evanston: Northwestern UP, 1968. Print.

Mintz, Sidney, and Richard Price. *The Birth of African American Culture.* Boston: Beacon, 1976. Print.

Molnár, Gábor Tamás. "Antropológia és Fikcióelmélet (Geertz, Greenblatt, Giles Goat-Boy)." ["Anthropology and Theories of Fiction (Geertz, Greenblatt, Giles Goat-Boy)"]. *Antropológia és Irodalom: Egy Új Paradigma Keresése.* [Anthropology and Literature: Looking for a New Paradigm]. Debrecen: Csokonai, 2003. 43-53. Print.

Morris, Ann R., and Margaret M. Dunn. "Flora and Fauna in Hurston's Florida Novels." *Zora in Florida.* Ed. Steve Glassman and Kathryn Lee Seidel. Orlando: U of Central Florida P, 1991. Print.

Morrison, Toni. "Black Matters." *Playing in the Dark: Whiteness and Literary Imagination.* Cambridge: Harvard UP, 1992. 1-29. Print.

Munn, D. Nancy. "Excluded Spaces: The Figure in the Aboriginal Australian Aboriginal Landscape." *The Anthropology of Space and Place: Locating Culture.* Ed. D. Low, Setha M., and Denise Lawrence-Zúñiga. Malden: Blackwell, 2003. 92-110.

Murphy, Joseph M. *Working the Spirit: Ceremonies of the African Diaspora.* Boston: Beacon, 1994. Print.

Newman Phillips, Evelyn. "'Doing More than Heads': African American Women Healing, Resisting, and Uplifting Others in St. Petersburg, Florida." *Frontiers* 22.2 (2001): n. pag. Web. 20 July 2008.

Norberg-Schulz, Christian. *Genius Loci. Towards a Phenomenology of Architecture.* London: Academy Editions, 1980. Print.

Ong, Walter J. *Orality and Literacy: The Technologizing of the Word.* London: Routledge, 2002. Print.

Osborne, Peter. "Non-Places and the Spaces of Art." *Journal of Architecture* 6 (Summer 2001): 183-94. Print.

Otto, Rudolf. *The Idea of the Holy: An Inquiry into the Non-Rational Factor in the Idea of the Divine and Its Relation to the Rational.* Trans. John W. Harvey. London: Oxford UP, 1958. Print.

Park, Deborah C. "Disability Studies in Human Geography." *Progress in Human Geography* 22.2 (1998): 208-33. Print.

Parker Pearson, Michael, and Colin Richards. *Architecture and Order: Approaches to Social Space.* London: Routledge, 1996. Print.

Pavlíc, Edward M. *Crossroads Modernism: Descent and Emergence in African-American Literary Culture.* Minneapolis: U of Minnesota P, 2002. Print.

---. "Syndetic Redemption: Above-Underground Emergence in David Bradley's 'The Chaneysville Incident.'" *African American Review* 30 (1996): n. pag. *Questia.* Web. 19 Nov. 2007.

Pellow, Deborah. "The Architecture of Female Seclusion in West Africa." *The Anthropology of Space and Place: Locating Culture.* Ed. D. Low, Setha

M., and Denise Lawrence-Zúñiga. Malden: Blackwell, 2003. 160-85. Print.

Peterson, Carla L. "Secular and Sacred Space in the Spiritual Autobiographies of Jarena Lee." *Reconfigured Spheres: Feminist Explorations of Literary Space.* Ed. Margaret R. Higonnet and Joan Templeton. Amherst, MA.: U of Massachusetts P, 1994. 37-60. Print.

Plant, Deborah G. *Every Tub Must Sit on Its Own Bottom: The Philosophy and Politics of Zora Neale Hurston.* Urbana: U of Illinois P, 1995. Print.

Polk, Noel. *Outside the Southern Myth.* Jackson, Mis.: UP of Mississippi, 1997. Print.

Pratt, Geraldine, and Brenda Yeoh. "Transnational (Counter) Topographies." *Gender, Place and Culture* 10.2 (2003): 159-66. Print.

Quashie, Kevin Everod. *Black Women, Identity, and Cultural Theory: (Un)becoming the Subject.* New Brunswick, NJ.: Rutgers UP, 2004. *Questia.* Web. 28 Nov. 2007.

Rapport, Nigel, and Joanna Overing. *Social and Cultural Anthropology: The Key Concepts.* London, New York: Routledge, 2000. Print.

Roberts, John W. *From Trickster to Badman: The Black Folk Hero in Slavery and Freedom.* Philadelphia: U of Pennsylvania P, 1989. Print.

Rosaldo, Renato. "Grief and a Headhunter's Rage." *Anthropological Theory: An Introductory History.* Ed. R. Jon McGee and Richard L. Warms. Mountain View: Mayfield, 1996. 483-97. Print.

Rose, Gillian. *Feminism and Geography: The Limits of Geographical Knowledge.* Minneapolis: U of Minnesota P, 1993. Print.

Ryan, Judylyn. "Water from an Ancient Well: The Recuperation of Double-Consciousness." Diss. U of Wisconsin, 1990. Print.

Russel, Kathy et al. *The Color Complex: The Politics of Skin Color among African Americans.* New York: Doubleday, 1992. Print.

Sadala, Maria Lucia Araujo, and Rubens de Camargo Ferreira Adorno. "Phenomenology as a Method to Investigate the Experience Lived: a Perspective from Husserl and Merleau Ponty's Thought." *Journal of Advanced Nursing* 37.3 (2002): 282–93. Print.

Sartre, Jean-Paul. *Being and Nothingness: A Phenomenological Essay on Ontology.* 1943. Trans. Hazel E. Barnes. New York: Washington Square, 1992. Print.

Sartre, Jean-Paul. *Critique of Dialectical Reason, Vol. 1. Basic Writings.* Ed. Stephen Priest. New York: Routledge, 2000. Print.

Schatzki, Theodore R. "Subject, Body, Place." *Annals of the Association Of American Geographers* 91.4 (2001): 698-702. Print.

Sheldrake, Philip. *Spaces for the Sacred: Place, Memory, and Identity.* Baltimore: John Hopkins UP, 2001. Print.

Siemerling, Winfried. *The New North American Studies: Culture, Writing and the Politics of Re/cognition*. New York: Routledge, 2004. Print.

Simms, Rupert. "Controlling Images and the Gender Construction of Enslaved African Women." *Gender and Society* 15.6 (2001): 879-97. Print.

Singh, Amritjit et al., eds. Introduction. *Memory and Cultural Politics: New Approaches to American Ethnic Literatures*. Boston: Northeastern UP, 1996. 3-19. Print.

Smitherman, Geneva. *Talkin That Talk: Language, Culture, and Education in African America*. New York: Routledge, 2000. *Questia*. Web. 25 July 2008.

Soja, Edward W. *Postmodern Geographies: The Reassertion of Space in Critical Theory*. London: Verso, 1989. Print.

---. *Thirdspace: Journeys to Los Angeles and Other Real-and-Imagined Places*. Malden: Blackwell, 1996. Print.

Sorensen, Leif. "Modernity on a Global Stage: Hurston's Alternative Modernism." *MELUS* 30.4 (2005): 3-24. *Questia*. Web. 17 June 2007.

Stein, Rachel. "Remembering the Sacred Tree: Black Women, Nature, and Voodoo in Zora Neale Hurston's *Tell My Horse* and *Their Eyes Were Watching God*. *Women's Studies* 25 (1996): 465-82. Print.

Steinberg, Theodore. *Acts of God: The Unnatural History of Natural Disaster in America*. New York: Oxford UP, 2000. Print.

Steinke, Peter L. "From Non-Place to Third Place." *The Clergy Journal* 84.7 (May/Jun2008): 3-4. Web. 17 Oct. 2008.

Stepto, Robert B. *From Behind the Veil: A Study of Afro-American Narrative*, Urbana: U of Illinois P, 1979. Print.

Stock, Brian. "Reading, Community and a Sense of Place." *Place/Culture/Representation*. Ed. James Duncan and David Ley. New York: Routledge, 1993. 134-328. Print.

Tallman, Janet. "The Ethnographic Novel: Finding the Insider's Voice." *Between Anthropology and Literature: Interdisciplinary Discourse*. Ed. Rose De Angelis. London: Routledge, 2002. 11-22.

The Holy Bible, New International Version (NIV). *Bible.org*. Web. 15 Dec. 2007.

---, King James Version (KJV). *Bible.org*. Web. 15 Dec. 2007.

Thiboutot, C. et al. "Gaston Bachelard and Phenomenology: Outline of a Theory of the Imagination." *Journal of Phenomenological Psychology* 30.1 (1999): 1-17. *Ebsco*. Web. 12 May 2006.

Thomson, Ian. "What Use Is the *Genius Loci*?" *Constructing Place: Mind and Matter*. Ed. Sarah Menin. New York: Routledge, 2003. 66-77. *Questia*. Web. 28 May 2008.

Trombold, John. "The Minstrel Show Goes to the Great War: Zora Neale Hurston's Mass Cultural Other." *MELUS* 24.1 (1999): 85-107. Print.

Tuan, Yi-Fu. *Space and Place: The Perspective of Experience*. Minneapolis: U of Minnesota P, 1977. Print.

Turner, Victor. *The Ritual Process*. New York: Aldine De Gruyter, 1995. Print.

Van Gennep, Arnold. *Übergangsriten*. [The Rites of Passage]. Frankfurt: Campus, 1986. Print.

Vizenor, Gerald Robert. *Manifest Manners: Postindian Warriors of Survivance*. Middletown: Wesleyan UP, 1993. Print.

Walker, Alice. "In Search of Zora Neale Hurston." *Ms.* 3 (March 1975): 4-9. Print.

Washington, Mary Helen. "A Woman Half in Shadow." *Zora Neale Hurston*. Ed. Harold Bloom. New York: Chelsea, 1986. 123-39. Print.

Wasserstrom, Steven M. *Religion after Religion: Gershom Scholem, Mircea Eliade, and Henry Corbin at Eranos*. Princeton: Princeton UP, 1999. Print.

Weathers, Glenda B. "Biblical Trees, Biblical Deliverance: Literary Landscapes of Zora Neale Hurston and Toni Morrison." *African American Review* 39.1-2 (2005): 201-12. *Questia*. Web. 12 Dec. 2007.

Wedam, Elfriede. "The 'Religious District' of Elite Congregations: Reproducing Spatial Centrality and Redefining Mission." *Sociology of Religion* 64.1 (2003): 47-64. Print.

West, Geneviewe. *Zora Neale Hurston and American Literary Culture*. Gainesville: UP of Florida, 2005. Print.

Wigley, Mark. "Untitled: The Housing of Gender." *Sexuality and Space*. Ed. Beatriz Colomina. New York: Princeton Architectural P, 1992. 327-89. Print.

Williams, Delores S. *Sisters in The Wilderness: The Challenge of Womanist God-Talk*. New York: Orbis, 1993. Print.

Wollan, Gjermund. "Heidegger's Philosophy of Space and Place." *Norwegian Journal of Geography* 57 (2003): 31-39. Print.

Wright, Richard. "Between Laughter and Tears." *Richard Wright: Books and Writers*. Ed. Michel Fabre. Jackson: UP of Mississippi, 1990. 250-51. Print.

Zimm, Malin. "The Dying Dreamer: Architecture of Parallel Realities." *Technoetic Arts* 1.1 (2003): 61-68. Print.

Index

Debrecener Studien zur Literatur

Herausgegeben von Tamás Lichtmann

www.peterlang.de

Peter Lang · Internationaler Verlag der Wissenschaften

Catharine Walker Bergström

Intuition of an Infinite Obligation

Narrative Ethics and Postmodern Gnostics in the Fiction of E. L. Doctorow

Frankfurt am Main, Berlin, Bern, Bruxelles, New York, Oxford, Wien, 2010.
189 pp.
Anglo-American studies. Edited by Rüdiger Ahrens and Kevin Cope. Vol. 38
ISBN 978-3-631-58749-2 · hardback € 47,80*

Grounded in theoretical studies of postmodern and narrative ethics, this book proposes the need for a re-examination of E. L. Doctorow's work from an ethical perspective. Through in-depth analyses of previously neglected intertexts, it questions the classification of his fiction as an expression of postmodern skepticism. Seven of Doctorow's most widely acclaimed novels are dealt with in chronological order, tracing his finely tuned characterizations of the human quest for narrative truth. Growing out of the early protagonists' vague sense of moral consciousness is their recognition of an obligation to interpret signs from and for the Other. Through logical deliberation and close reading, the study gradually identifies the narrative voice of the post-modern gnostic.

Content: E. L. Doctorow · Narrative ethics · Postmodern ethics · Intuition · Polyphonic Narrative · Historiography · Quest for truth · Infinite obligation · Levinas · The Other · Identity · The Self · Emerson · Self-reliance · The Over-Soul · Jung · Collective unconscious · Synchronicity · Gnosticism · Gnosis · Kabbalah · Hope · Scepticism · Derrida · Deconstruction · Intertextuality · Welcome to Hard Times · Book of Daniel · Ragtime · Loon Lake · Billy Bathgate · Waterworks · City of God

Frankfurt am Main · Berlin · Bern · Bruxelles · New York · Oxford · Wien
Distribution: Verlag Peter Lang AG
Moosstr. 1, CH-2542 Pieterlen
Telefax 00 41 (0) 32 / 376 17 27

*The €-price includes German tax rate
Prices are subject to change without notice
Homepage http://www.peterlang.de